The Top 50 R
Romantic P. _____

How to avoid the Narcissist's Trap

CW01558633

Author: Maria McMahon, BSc. (Psych. (Hons)), Dip. H.E.NLP/Hyp

Cover Design: Sharon Brownlie

Copyright© 2019 Maria McMahon

Acknowledgements

I'd like to thank my priceless friends and fellow authors/bloggers, Else Byskov and Kaye A. Peters for proof reading and commenting on the first draft. Also, thanks to a special lady and survivor/thriver of narcissistic abuse, Sue K. – I am so grateful to you, even though you don't want any credit! If there are any errors in this book, they will be mine.

Ida Wonders, a very special friend and advocate for victims of narcissistic abuse. Thank you for reading the first draft and making some excellent points which helped make this a better book. And thank you for sharing some of your experience with a narcissist in the Foreword of this book. I am so grateful to you for your insights, generosity and friendship.

My launch team – too numerous to mention but you know who you are and you have my sincere thanks and gratitude.

The authors who kindly gave me permission to quote from their work. My knowledge of NPD and Abuse has expanded exponentially because of your expertise and dedication to sharing your knowledge with the world. It is much-needed.

All the women and men in my Facebook Groups, for sharing so many of your stories with me, for permission to use some of your experiences in this book and for your courage. You inspire me!

And finally, to the many pioneering men and women who are championing the cause and helping people to understand and heal from narcissistic abuse with their books, blogs, YouTube Channels and Social Media presence. The list is long and you can find some of them in the Reading and Resources Section at the end of this book.

Dedication

To everyone who has suffered the abomination that is narcissistic abuse, I hope this book will help you to never fall into the narcissist's trap again.

TABLE OF CONTENTS

Who is affected by NPD?

Is it only women who are affected?

How widespread is NPD and abuse?

So what happens when you meet a Narcissist?

CHAPTER TWO

THE TOP 50 RED FLAGS OF THE ROMANTIC PREDATOR – aka THE NARCISSIST

INITIAL MEETING/EARLY DAYS:
RED FLAG Nos 1 to 19

Red Flag No 1:
Not trusting your intuition!

Red Flag No 2:
Judging a book by its cover

Red Flag No 3:
Powerful sexual attraction

Red Flag No 4:
love bombing – Please, for the love of God, don't fall for it!

Red Flag No 5:
Emotional Seduction – love bombing by a different name

Red Flag No 6:
They seem to 'instinctively' know a LOT about you!

Red Flag No 7:
They brag, boast and name-drop

Red Flag No 8:
They want to know EVERYTHING about you

Red Flag No 9:
They want to know NOTHING about you

Red Flag No 10:
They are alone – but why?

Red Flag No 11:
They trash their Exes

Red Flag No 12:
They have no respect for your boundaries

Red Flag No 13:
They have an explanation for everything!

Red Flag No 14:
YOU are a Red Flag… if you're an Empath or Highly Sensitive Person (HSP) – 10 Common Traits

Red Flag No 15:
You had an abusive childhood, or have Narcissistic Parent/s

Red flag No 16:
You're my Soul Mate. It's destiny!

Red Flag No 17:
They want to meet your family/friends BUT their family is a different story

Red Flag No 18:
They have no solid/long-term friendships

They're always checking their phones / furtive with computers

Red Flag No 28:
They're jealous and controlling

Red Flag No 29:
The mask is off! 8 ways they start devaluing you

Red Flag No 30:
Gaslight-ning Strikes – and you don't know what hit you!

Red Flag No 31:
Narcissists are Supreme Blame-Shifters

Red Flag No 32:
Projection

Red Flag No 33:
They create and thrive on chaos

Red Flag No 34:
They are pathological liars

Red Flag No 35:
Sex becomes a nightmare

Red Flag No 36:
They ruin every social occasion for you

Red Flag No 37:
The Silent Treatment/Stonewalling/Ghosting

Red Flag No 38:
Triangulation: Positive and Negative

Red Flag No 39:

They cheat on you

Red Flag No 40:
They isolate you from family and friends

CHAPTER FIVE

THE BIG RED FLAGS OF NARCISSISTIC ABUSE:
RED FLAG Nos 41-50

Red Flag No 41:
Cognitive Dissonance

Red Flag No 42:
Toxic Shame/Guilt

Red Flag No 43:
Trauma Bonding

Red Flag No 44:
Narcissistic Abuse is ruining your health

Red Flag No 45:
Narcissists Discard you like Trash!

Red Flag No 46: Flying Monkeys

Red Flag No 47:
Smear Campaigns

Red Flag No 48:
Hoovering – The Romantic Predator strikes again!

Red Flag No 49:
Love-Bombed, Devalued, Discarded... AGAIN

FOREWORD
by Ida Wonders

Narcissism exists on a spectrum from healthy narcissism to covert malignant narcissism. Having a relationship with a person with Narcissistic Personality Disorder is a one of a kind experience, maybe best compared to a journey into hell.

He said all the right things. He read my mind. He swept me off my feet, seemed to be original and charming and so into me. He effortlessly tapped into my deepest longings, fears and thoughts. We laughed a lot, he seemed so romantic and enthusiastic, hungry for life and for love. I never fell for anyone so fast. Eventually I had to realise that I had fallen for a ghost. The person I saw in him never existed. He had moved in with a plan to control, deceive and destroy, I never had a chance because I couldn't read the signs. Actually, I knew some red flags from previous experience; right from the start I told him I would never let anyone get between me and my friends. Never would I let anyone isolate me ever again. He reacted like the narcissist he is: he mirrored me. For a few seconds there was a puzzled look on his face, then he caught himself and told me he knew exactly what I was talking about: it had happened to him as well!

The part of me that was so hurt and refused to grow up (this is to you, my adorably frolicsome and cheerful inner child, I love you!) also refused to believe that someone could be going all out to harm me while being friendly and charming, caring and apparently all engaged in making me happy. And telling me he loved me. The stories a narcissist will tell you to win you over and control you are beyond belief unless you have educated yourself on how to debunk them. The faster the better. Unless you learn to unmask them right away, you are still in danger of being gaslighted. That is why I find this book so incredibly valuable and feel very honoured that Maria has asked me to write this preface.

The last narcissist I was involved with has certainly regretted ever picking up with me. I have changed his life in ways he had never dreamt of. And the experience has also changed my life - but in contrast to his life, mine has become better than ever. Not that I owe him for that! It was all because I seized the opportunity to change my life once and for all. He was the last Narc I got involved with and it will stay that way.

One of the wonderful people who helped me to break the Trauma Bond and overcome the harmful emotional patterns of the past is Maria. In a one-hour online session she freed me of a flashback that had been tormenting me. It felt like magic to me! I decided to work with her. I knew I could trust her completely. The break-through session we had felt like a long, long journey but in real life it lasted probably not much longer than two hours. It was deep and painful but liberating. The anxiety attacks and unpredictable mood swings that had been haunting me all my life disappeared for good. I can now experience my sadness and fears without panicking. Maria and I have created a safe place to go to, a place of self-integration, self-understanding and self-love. Emotions come and go. No narcissist will ever be able to exploit my emotions and use them against me again.

To see someone break free from narcissistic abuse, to learn the lessons this experience wants to teach us and to rise to freedom and self-love is one of the things that makes me truly happy and fills my heart with joy and satisfaction. I will remain involved in helping to raise awareness about narcissistic abuse and to help those affected by it to seize this opportunity, take back their power and become fully who they are meant to be.

Thank you, Maria, for what you have done for me, for your dedication, and for making this world a better place through your healing work.

Ida Wonders, founder of the Facebook Group, The Dopamine Diaries

The Top 50 Red Flags of Romantic Predators

How to avoid the Narcissist's Trap

"If you know what to look for, you can save yourself from the nightmare of narcissistic abuse. Prevention is WAY better than cure."
Maria McMahon

"The thorn on the stem can still draw blood from the hand that holds the rose."
Kaye A Peters

CHAPTER ONE

THE BASICS OF NARCISSISM

Introduction

Narcissistic abuse seems to be everywhere you look these days and if you are unfortunate enough to have been involved with a narcissist who masqueraded as a romantic knight in shining armor or a goddess on a white horse when you met, only to have discovered that behind the shiny façade lay a dark, manipulative, evil monster, then this book is for you. It's for you because you never want to get involved with another narcissist again as long as you live, and you want to arm yourself with all the knowledge you can to help you protect yourself from falling into the same trap in the future.

The biggest tragedy about narcissistic abuse is that you never hear of it until it's way too late and you're deeply entrenched in a relationship that's destroying you and you don't know what the hell is going on. So you Google various phrases and eventually you come across the term 'narcissist', and suddenly all the pieces start falling into place as you realize that you're dealing with one. There is no reason why you would have heard of it otherwise. Even therapists often haven't heard of it! So how can you protect yourself from something you never knew existed?

There are hundreds of excellent books out there on Narcissistic Personality Disorder (NPD) and abuse and thousands of blog articles, yet I couldn't find a definitive resource that would help you to easily spot the well-worn tactics of the Romantic Predator, i.e., those huge Red Flags that show up time and time again. When you spend as much time as I do as a Clinical NLP / Hypnotherapist, dealing with people who are suffering with the aftermath of this abuse, you hear the same stories happening to innocent, unsuspecting people over and over again. I therefore, came to know a great many of the top Red Flags that, **had you known about them,** could have saved you from falling into the Romantic Predator's slick, seductive trap.

During my research (which basically never stops), I could only find one book that actually had 'Red Flags' and anything to do with Narcissism in the title. That book was 'Red Flag: 50 Warning Signs of Narcissistic Seduction', by prolific author and self-aware Narcissist (or 'Greater Elite' or 'Ultra Elite' Narcissist' as he defines himself – more on this later), HG Tudor. I've read more books than I can remember on NPD abuse, recovery and healing, and Tudor is one of only two 'Self-Aware' Narcissists I know of whose body of work provides invaluable insight from the perspective of the perpetrator himself. I've read several of his books (he's written over 50) and they are jaw-dropping, shocking and enlightening. The other is Sam Vaknin, whose book 'Malignant Self-Love: Narcissism Revisited', is now in its 10th Edition.

Of course, I've read Tudor's Red Flags book and can attest to the reality of what he has written, because I'm hearing it from the other side... from the victims who fall into the traps, again and again. I run two Facebook support groups, have a Public Page and work with clients who are trying to recover from the abuse, so I am seeing the fallout, firsthand, every day. I have no compunction in calling Narcissists the scourge of the earth, because they are. Yet there is a part of me that feels sadness for them, because they are desperately unhappy, broken souls. That does not, however, mean that I have any sympathy for them. I don't. The damage they knowingly do to innocent people is unforgivable. I decided to write this book to help people to know what to look for, to be able to rapidly identify the most common 'Red Flags' and give them the knowledge and tools to effectively avoid the Romantic Predator.

I know how much pain this abuse causes and the pain you have to endure is excruciating, so if there is a way to save you from having this happen to you, I'm totally on board with that. I believe prevention is absolutely better than cure. When you understand why you've attracted them, what they are looking for and most importantly, your own vulnerabilities and the crucial part they play, you can protect yourself and never let it happen to you again.

This book could be 10 times longer than it is, because the rabbit hole of Narcissistic Personality Disorder and the abuse it causes is so deep. It is a vast and complex field, and I have striven to keep it as simple and straightforward as possible. I want you to be able to easily remember the flags and not be bogged down by complex psychology and neuroscience. I make only the briefest references to these where I feel they are helpful. I want to also point out that this book is not about healing and recovering from narcissistic abuse – that will be my next one! This one is about helping you to learn and spot the Red Flags in the first place and avoid the pain altogether.

If this book helps just ONE person to never fall for a narcissist again, I will be happy, but it is my dearest wish it will save many more people from the narcissist's trap. So yes, shameless plug here – if you find this book helpful, please leave a review on your favourite book platform. Please share it on your social media and any groups you are in that deal with narcissistic abuse. Nobody gets rich from book sales... that is not my aim. My aim is to do everything I can to help prevent more people from being hurt beyond belief by the toxicity that is NPD, and sharing this book with them could help. In doing so, you will have helped save someone, and you'll have my eternal gratitude.

How to get the most out of this book

I realize you could be just about anywhere in your understanding of narcissistic abuse. You could be:

- Brand new to it and have only just come across the term but know or suspect that you have been or are currently, involved with a narcissist

- Aware that you have a pattern of attracting toxic people and are desperate to avoid this happening to you AGAIN

- Back on the dating scene, hoping to meet the man or woman of your dreams, after too many failed relationships, but worried that you don't know what to look out for

- Absolutely clueless about how or why you attracted a narcissist

- Know what narcissists are but still falling into their traps and you don't know why or how to protect yourself

- In a relationship at the moment but not sure if you're being 'abused'

- Currently in a relationship with a narcissist and desperately trying to figure out how you got there, and how to get out

- Aware there are 'Red Flags' but not sure what they are

This book will answer all the questions you have about Red Flags and how the romantic predator uses them to trap YOU.

I'll show you how to spot them, understand WHY you keep attracting them, and I will give you solid advice every step of the way, on how to protect yourself and stop it from happening again. This book will also clarify, if you are in any doubt, whether you are in an abusive relationship. I also hope it will give you the courage to start planning your exit strategy to get out and live your life in newfound freedom and joy. So read this book carefully, from cover to cover. Have a notebook and pen with you when you do, and make notes on:

- Areas that resonate and ring bells for you

- Areas that point to your particular vulnerabilities
- Red Flags you've experienced or are currently experiencing
- How this relationship is making you feel if you're currently in one or still struggling to process the pain of being discarded
- Anything else that comes up for you

Make notes on and know that learning the Top 50 Red Flags will prevent you from making the same mistakes again. If you are knee-deep in a narcissistic relationship now, I want you to know there is a way out and you can find it. In spite of how prevalent narcissistic abuse is, people are leaving, healing and recovering every day. I am seeing the evidence of this with people in my groups and with clients I work with all the time, so please take courage and know that you too, can heal and thrive after abuse.

If you've been in several narcissistic relationships and just don't understand why you keep ending up in the same abusive situation, albeit with a different person each time, this book will shed light on some of the possible reasons and I hope, give you the clarity and insight you need to recognize your own patterns, vulnerability, and how to protect yourself from future Narc Attacks.

Now, it's important to note, not all the flags I've covered will apply to all Romantic Predators – aka narcissists - because different types of narcissist have different methods of seduction. What you need is to be aware of these flags so when they show up, warning bells will start ringing in your ears and you'll know to pay attention.

Not everyone you meet will be a narcissist, so you don't want to 'throw the baby out with the bathwater'. Give each new person a chance to show who they are. But when you start seeing the flags showing up, you can put yourself on high alert. This is when self-protection needs to kick in and you need to start being very careful. The purpose of this book is primarily to help you know how to spot and avoid the narcissist's trap. Where possible, I've tried to give you the best advice I can. Creating this book was a very logical way for me to help you not get hurt in the first place.

I've grouped the flags into stages: Those stages include covering the Initial Meeting/Early Days, Getting Deeper into the Relationship, Devaluing and the BIG Red Flags of Narcissistic abuse. These flags are not in any particular order, other than the 'Initial Meeting' and Red Flag No 1 because it is THE most important one of all. Any one of them or more usually a combination thereof will show up pretty quickly if this person is a narcissist. This is a no-holds-barred book. Everything I've written here has happened to either a client I've worked with, someone in my group or other groups I'm a member of, or someone I've connected with in my network. This s*** is happening to people every single day. It's not scaremongering. Don't ever underestimate the narcissist , because they are capable of anything. Even murder... or at the very least, plotting to have you murdered.

I recommend you read the entire book and then go back over it. After the initial reading, a lot of the jigsaw pieces of narcissistic predation and the subsequent abuse will fit into place for you. You will see the picture much more clearly. In order to protect yourself from narcissists and the horrendous psychological abuse they will subject you to, you must learn everything you can about this virulent, toxic form of abuse. This is the only way you can protect yourself from future 'Narc Attacks'. I always say, 'Knowledge is Power', because it's your most potent defense weapon against a narcissist.

So, before I get started on the 50 Red Flags, and in case you're very new to NPD and narcissistic abuse, I'm going to briefly cover some key essentials that you will need to know. This is by no means an extensive exposé of narcissism. It's a huge subject, so I'm just going to cover the basics and if you want to dig deeper, I've added a Reading and Resources Section at the end of this book. Narcissists are colloquially referred to as narcs so I sometimes refer to them that way too.

What is Narcissistic Personality Disorder (NPD)?

The term Narcissism originated from Greek Mythology where a handsome young hunter, Narcissus, fell in love with his own reflection in a pool of water and, unable to tear himself away from this mesmerizing visage, he stayed there gazing at himself until he died. Upon which, a flower grew beside him. The flower is Narcissus, more commonly known as Daffodil or Jonquil. I'm wondering what the flower was called before it became known as Narcissus!

Coming back to reality, the Diagnostic and Statistical Manual of Mental Disorders, Fifth Edition, (DSM-5), published by the American Psychiatric Association, classifies NPD as one of the Cluster B Mental Disorders, which is determined by the presence of 9 personality traits; however, only 5 of them need to be present to diagnose NPD. Those are listed below for the record. I think No 7 needs revision because 'lacks empathy' is a gross underestimation. Narcissists don't 'lack' empathy. According to bestselling author, speaker and all-round expert on narcissistic abuse, Kim Saeed, the 'Narcissist's Lack of Empathy is a Myth'. She points out that it's compassion, remorse and regret that they lack and that 'a person can understand what another person feels, thinks and experiences without feeling the human emotions that go along with it.' This is of course exactly what narcissists do when they mirror their targets and employ the addition of Cognitive Empathy – which is a skill that can be learned that basically allows them to fake empathy to achieve their own ends. More on Cognitive Empathy later. But here are the DSM-5 Traits for NPD:

1. Has a grandiose sense of self-importance (e.g., exaggerates achievements and talents, expects to be recognized as superior without commensurate achievements).

2. Is preoccupied with fantasies of unlimited success, power, brilliance, beauty, or ideal love.
3. Believes that he or she is "special" and unique and can only be understood by, or should associate with, other special or high-status people (or institutions).
4. Requires excessive admiration.
5. Has a sense of entitlement, i.e., unreasonable expectations of especially favorable treatment or automatic compliance with his or her expectations.
6. Is interpersonally exploitative, i.e., takes advantage of others to achieve his or her own ends.
7. Lacks empathy: is unwilling to recognize or identify with the feelings and needs of others.
8. Is often envious of others or believes that others are envious of him or her.
9. Shows arrogant, haughty behaviors or attitudes.

Throughout this book, you'll see these traits showing up in many different forms. Check as you're reading to see which ones you can spot as you go through them when we get to the Red Flags. Every type of narcissistic behavior will fit one or more of those traits. It's important to note, however, that NPD is on a spectrum, so the levels and intensity of traits can vary from person to person. It is generally agreed by every source I've ever researched that NP Disordered people are destructive to people they are closely involved with. This includes romantic partners, families, friends, and colleagues.

Types of Narcissists

There seems to be more and more variations on the theme of how many different 'types' of narcissist there are and an equally wide-ranging array of explanations of the types of characteristic traits that each one possesses. Some of the most common ones you're likely to come across are:

- Overts aka* Grandiose
- Coverts aka Closet Narcissists/Ultra/Elite/Greater
- Covert Malignant aka Toxic (but aren't they all?)
- Vulnerable aka Introverted, Shy, Victim
- Altruistic aka Communal or Prosocial (may be publicly giving generously to charities and appear humanitarian/philanthropic)
- Cerebral – all about their intelligence
- Somatic – all about physicality and beauty
- Elite – a combination of Cerebral and Somatic

*aka – also known as

You may also come across Histrionic Personality Disorder, Borderline Personality Disorder and Antisocial Personality Disorder. I will briefly cover these so you are aware of them also as there is often confusion around them.

So here's the 'Nutshell' version of the three most common types of Narcissists:

Overt Narcissists

- Big-headed, vain, loud, boastful
- Consider themselves brilliant, powerful and gorgeous
- Rude to anyone they perceive as beneath them
- No respect for boundaries, rules, authority or people
- Take credit where it's NOT due
- Exaggerate their skills, talents and accomplishments
- Obviously abusive, even in front of others, such as in the workplace
- Think they are perfect and beyond reproach
- Are shockingly egocentric
- Can be charming, charismatic, persuasive, clever, funny
- Can 'work the system', i.e. persuade and manipulate to get what they want
- Liars
- Can be hypersexual (if Somatic)
- Desperate for admiration and praise (whether deserved or not)
- Monsters behind closed doors

Covert Malignant Narcissists

- Charming, charismatic, persuasive, clever, funny
- Successful – or pretend to be or appear to be on the face of things
- Intelligent, cunning and manipulative
- Brilliant at hiding their true identity
- Totally lacking in empathy
- Selfish
- Egocentric
- Pathological liars
- Hypersexual

- The most dangerous of all Narcissists
- Monsters behind closed doors

Vulnerable Narcissists

- Quiet Smugness/Superiority
- Passive Aggressive Behavior
- Self-absorption
- Victim mentality
- Hyper-sensitivity to criticism or perceived criticism
- Lack of empathy (common to ALL narcissistic personalities)
- Inability to form close, genuine relationships
- Liars and also desperate for admiration and praise (whether deserved or not)
- Asexual or very low sex drive
- Monsters behind closed doors

It's also important to be aware of the distinction between a Cerebral and a Somatic, because they have different approaches to how they seduce you, but they are equally dangerous. The vulnerable narcissist is not going to be either cerebral or somatic, but there is a further category to be aware of, the 'Elite' narcissist, which I will also cover.

The Cerebral Narcissist

Cerebral narcissists are all about their own intelligence, and they often do have above-average intelligence. They will try to bedazzle everyone with their extensive knowledge of everything, and they'll always take the long, complicated highway to explain everything so they can display how brilliant and clever they are. They believe that they are God's gift to the world, and nobody surpasses them intellectually. Even if everyone within earshot is bored already, they won't notice, because they're always too wrapped up in their own dazzling brilliance to notice – or care if they were.

Superlative Language Skills

Cerebral narcissists use their language skills to impress... or to chew you up and spit you out. They can run rings around most people and you'll very soon get lost in the maze of their wordplay - often referred to as 'Word Salad' that comes out of their mouths. The way they do this is fascinating to behold. Trying to figure out how they get from A to Z in sentences is like trying to find your way out of a dark maze, blindfolded and with 15 loudspeakers giving you different directions. You have no chance of finding your way out of that maze!

Superiority

They also exhibit disdain for people they consider 'beneath' them in intellectual stature and they believe they should only associate with exceptional people – even though they don't really believe anyone is equal to them. Their victims will usually be highly intelligent – proving that yes, highly intelligent people can just as easily be hoodwinked and sucked in by a Narcissist as anyone. They are skillful manipulators. Watch how they behave around people such as waiters or shop staff. Usually you'll find if they are not outright rude, they'll be disdainful and don't want to give the time of day to such 'minions'. Their arrogance is often quite palpable and can leave you feeling very uncomfortable when they are rude, show-off or are demeaning to people who simply do not deserve this kind of treatment.

But, they may also pretend to be highly intelligent when in fact they are not. They just have grandiose ideas about their own brilliance. It's an ego-driven facade that they keep up, even to themselves.

No Sex, thank you!

When it comes to sex, they're totally the opposite of the Somatic narcissist, who uses sex as a weapon of seduction and destruction. The Cerebral Narcissist puts sex very low down on their list of priorities or avoids it altogether. They don't care so much for appearances and personal hygiene and often that's to make themselves less sexually appealing to their partners. They'll refuse to shower, change their underwear, socks or even brush their teeth.

So now let's look at the Somatic.

The Somatic Narcissist

Somatic narcissists are all about the physical and the beautiful. Appearance is everything. They want to look good and usually want to have someone who looks equally good on their arm; a trophy, as it were. Somatics flaunt their sex appeal, sensual/sexual prowess, and gorgeous bodies. They'll frequently brag about how many times people eye them up, chat them up, flirt with them and even sleep with them. Basically, they have a 'kiss and tell all' policy for anyone who will listen. Because they look so good and can be extremely charming, they have no trouble picking up their targets. They're experts at reeling you in. Unless you know what to look for.

Excessive concern or obsession about their appearance

They are constantly primping and preening themselves, are usually spotless, immaculate and very well turned out. You'll often catch them checking out their reflection. They love mirrors and shiny reflective surfaces that will give them extra glimpses of themselves. Yes, seriously, they do. They spend a lot of time at the gym. Nothing wrong with that, but if this is one of their traits among others here, watch out. The gym is an excellent place for them to legitimately flaunt their bodies. Fake tan and oil are not beyond the realms of possibility. All of these traits can be summed up in one simple word: Vanity. Somatics are extremely vain people.

Materialistic

Somatics are very materialistic and need status symbols to flaunt their greatness. They like to wear high-end clothing and designer products. They drive expensive cars and live in posh neighborhoods, even if it puts them into huge debt. Remember, appearance is everything to them.

Hypersexual

Sex is used as a tool to capture and ensnare you in a way no other method can. And they are good at it. They know how to push your hot buttons and give you the best sex of your life. What you don't, and can't know, is that they are emotionally detached, even in the seeming throes of passion.

Self-Absorbed

Remember they are all about themselves, so every conversation is likely to be about them. They have a high sense of self-entitlement and hold such grandiose ideas about themselves, that you should sit listening in abject fascination, to everything that comes out of their mouths. Yet anything you say is brushed off, ignored, or you get only a cursory response and with lightning speed, the conversation loops right back to them.

The Elite Narcissist

A narcissist can be BOTH cerebral and somatic. I call it beauty and brains in one horrible, toxic package that is going to wreak havoc in your life. The aforementioned author HG Tudor is credited with creating this 'type' and you won't find references to it outside of his work. However, I think it's vitally important and you need to be aware that this type exists. The term 'Elite' in this context he defines as a cadre.* He has described himself as Elite, Greater narcissist, Ultra Elite and a Narcissistic Psychopath. However, during my email exchanges with him to request his permission to quote him, he clarified:

'I am an Ultra Elite Narcissist, since school and cadre are applicable.'

And in a subsequent email he further clarified:

'I am an Ultra, as one of a kind, which is a step up from the Greater. I have previously referred to myself as a Greater.'

He does not define himself as a covert malignant narcissist, but as he has been clinically diagnosed as a narcissist, and also refers to himself as a 'Narcissistic Psychopath' on his website, it's reasonable to assume he is definitely both covert (unlike Sam Vaknin, Tudor's real identity is unknown), and (his books leave you in no doubt) malignant. I think the important thing to understand is that unless you are familiar with his work, covert malignant narcissist would be the best fit for his 'type' from those you are likely to be more familiar with from the mainstream narrative, compared with any other type. However, I do acknowledge the much higher level of complexity and sophistication he brings to our understanding of narcissist types, NPD and abuse. The brushstrokes are much broader than any other writer I've come across.

*cadre: Tudor identifies 4: the Victim, the Somatic, the Cerebral and the Elite. He also refers to three different 'schools' – the Lesser, the Mid-Range and the Greater. On his website he clarifies that:

'Knowing what cadre and school your narcissist belongs to is extremely helpful in enabling you to understand why he or she behaves in the manner that they do and also to enable you to know what you need to do and what you should expect.'

His article, 'The Greater Narcissist – Five Facts', is both brilliant and chilling. He poses 5 questions and here I'm sharing (with his permission) a snippet from each answer, but I urge you to read the full article and I will put the link in the Reading and Resources Section. However, Tudor's work is brutally honest and can be very painful for those new to the world of NPD and abuse so if you're in an emotionally weak state, don't read it. I know many (women) who have tried but find his work too painful to deal with. Note that he is British so the British spelling applies.

1. Do We Know What We Are Doing?

'The Greater Narcissist is aware that he or she is different from other people. He or she knows that their emotional spectrum has been stunted or as we prefer to regard it, altered to achieve maximum efficiency in our machinations. The Greater Narcissist knows he operates in a different world to other people and revels in such a special status. He or she knows that they are superior, admired and feared.'

2. Do We Know We Hurt Others?

'Unlike the instinctive response of the Lesser Narcissist or the instinctive but more controlled moderate reaction of the Mid-Ranger, the Greater Narcissist knows that he or she is an instrument that inflicts pain. Whether it is the withdrawal of something wonderful or delightful or the imposition of something unpleasant and hateful the Greater Narcissist knows that they hurt.'

3. Do We Act Deliberately?

'Everything that is done by the Greater Narcissist is deliberate. The lesser responds as a matter of course... The Greater Narcissist regards the manipulation of others as a game and one which is enjoyable to engage in.'

4. Can We Control This Behaviour?

'Not only is the Greater Narcissist an expert in the control of others he exerts considerable control over his own behaviour. His higher functioning allows him considerable latitude to pass the blame onto others and feign an inability to control what he does.'

5. Can We Stop It?

'The Greater Narcissist could stop his or her behaviour owing to the degree of control that he or she is able to exert but whilst there *is the capability to stop this behaviour, both benign and malign, the Greater Narcissist will not do so.'*

The 'Elite' narcissist' is literally a combination of a very intelligent, very gorgeous person who is going to be extremely well equipped (in all departments!) to sweep you right off your feet and into the horrible world of narcissistic abuse. If you have the misfortune to meet a 'Greater' or 'Ultra' narcissist, you will really need to have your wits about you and know the Red Flags because they are a very dangerous breed. However, there is some good news! According to Mr. Tudor, only 0.5 percent of 'His Kind', are 'Greater' narcissists. And if he, as an 'Ultra', is 'one of a kind', then you've got very little chance of meeting one, but always be on the alert, especially if you meet someone who is seems super-slick in every way.

Monsters behind closed doors

If you meet a man (or woman) who exhibits all the traits of the 'Elite', watch out! Watch like a hawk - and leave them before things get really started. Because the further into the relationship you get, the harder it will be to break out and the more damage they will do to you. Behind closed doors, they ALL soon show their true colors and will make your life a complete misery, no matter which 'flavor' they are.

You might have noticed that I've put 'Monsters behind closed doors' at the end of each list of traits above. That's because they may have different tactics in their approaches to seduction, but ultimately, their end game is always the same. No matter what 'type' the narcissist is, the bottom line is that they are all essentially the same in that they want to emotionally destroy you as this is their means of attaining their own ends and satiating their appetite for narcissistic supply or 'fuel' as it's also known. Their appetite IS insatiable. You will never be enough, no matter what you do, and you can and will tie yourself into knots trying, but it will still never, ever be enough and they will eventually discard you and move on to their next target, leaving you emotionally destroyed, depressed and a shadow of your former self. This WILL happen to you if you let it.

If you discard them, woe betide you because this is going to cause narcissistic injury, rage, and will very likely result in them starting a seriously nasty Smear Campaign against you. If you've been through even one narcissistic relationship, you will already know, to your very painful cost, the truth of this irrefutable fact. This book's aim is to help you to spot the Red Flags and NOT let this happen to you.

Antisocial Personality Disorder, Borderline Personality Disorder and
Histrionic Personality Disorder (HPD)

Though the focus of this book is purely on NPD, I want to briefly mention these other personality disorders, as there is often confusion about whether a person is narcissistic, histrionic, borderline or antisocial personality disordered. In addition to NPD, these 3 make up the four Cluster B Personality Disorders on the DSM-5.

The American Psychiatric Association characterizes them as follows:

Antisocial personality disorder: a pattern of disregarding or violating the rights of others. A person with antisocial personality disorder may not conform to social norms, may repeatedly lie or deceive others or may act impulsively.

APD is determined by the presence of these 8 traits:

1. Violation of the physical or emotional rights of others
2. Lack of stability in job and home life
3. Irritability and aggression

4. Lack of remorse
5. Consistent irresponsibility
6. Recklessness, impulsivity
7. Deceitfulness
8. A childhood diagnosis (or symptoms consistent with) conduct disorder

People in this category (statistically more men than women) tend to get involved in petty crimes, substance abuse and often, more serious criminal behavior as they grow to adulthood. None of which behaviors are unheard of in narcissists. Alcoholism and drug abuse are also very common.

Borderline Personality Disorder: a pattern of instability in personal relationships, intense emotions, poor self-image and impulsivity. A person with borderline personality disorder may go to great lengths to avoid being abandoned, have repeated suicide attempts, display inappropriate intense anger or have ongoing feelings of emptiness.

BPD is determined by the presence of these 9 traits:

1. Fear of abandonment
2. Unstable relationships
3. Unclear or shifting self-image
4. Impulsive, self-destructive behaviors
5. Self-harm
6. Extreme emotional swings
7. Chronic feelings of emptiness
8. Explosive anger

Many of these traits could be applicable to the vulnerable narcissist, particularly fear of abandonment, unclear or shifting self-image, self-harm, and chronic feelings of emptiness, which all play well with the personality profile of a vulnerable (or Shy/Victim) narcissist.

Histrionic personality disorder: a pattern of excessive emotion and attention seeking. People with histrionic personality disorder may be uncomfortable when they are not the center of attention, may use physical appearance to draw attention to themselves or have rapidly shifting or exaggerated emotions.

HPD (DSM-5) is determined by the presence of the 9 following traits:

1. Self-centeredness, feeling uncomfortable when not the center of attention
2. Constantly seeking reassurance or approval
3. Inappropriately seductive appearance or behavior
4. Rapidly shifting emotional states that appear shallow to others
5. Overly concerned with physical appearance and using physical appearance to draw attention to self
6. Opinions are easily influenced by other people, but difficult to back up with details
7. Excessive dramatics with exaggerated displays of emotion
8. Tendency to believe that relationships are more intimate than they actually are
9. Is highly suggestible (easily influenced by others)

Looking at the brief descriptions/traits of all these disorders, you can see how they can become confused as traits in Antisocial, Borderline and Histrionic ALL show up at times in narcissists. The fact is that HPD often co-occurs with BPD and NPD; to the point that some experts believe that HPD is indistinguishable from BPD. I think this is too broad a brushstroke however, having spent 7 years in a relationship with a BPD myself: he never demonstrated any signs of HPD.

If you compare those to the 9 of HPD to NPD, you'll see there are similarities and differences. HPDs tend to show up as 'Drama Queens', full of theatrics and are easily influenced, have no strong opinions of their own and are shallow and 'needy'. The traits that make a narcissist so deadly are missing. But if you get a person who has a combination of HPD and NPD, then you will be dealing with an explosive, histrionic narcissist.

What makes a Narcissist?

The exact causes of how NPD develops are still unknown, but several theories – biologic, psychological, social and environmental factors have merit, and all undoubtedly play a role in one way or another. As this is a vast and complex subject requiring a book of its own, I'm going to make this very brief and mention the most common theories.

Dysfunctional/Abusive Parents

We know from years of research that an abusive childhood often leads to that child either becoming an abuser or becoming the abused. Narcissists may become so because of such dysfunctional parenting. If they are constantly devalued and abused, they may develop coping mechanisms that shut them off from being able to develop normally. They may create a fake persona, fantasy world, or both, to shield themselves from the harsh realities they are dealing with. This fake world becomes more real to them and they want to keep this false reality at all costs. If their parent(s) are also narcissistic, this can have a huge influence because children subconsciously model their parents' behavior.

Overindulgent Parents

On the other end of the spectrum, overindulgent parents can be to blame. If a child is treated like a little Prince or Princess from a very early age, by parents who want their child to think he or she is perfect, can do no wrong and is entitled to everything they want, that child will develop a distorted view of themselves and their place in the world. Such children are basically spoiled rotten and never chastised, so they never learn the basic ground rules for good behavior. They often turn into narcissists because they've never learned to respect other people's feelings or needs. They grow up thinking they are superior to everyone else and develop an overblown sense of entitlement – a trait common in all narcissists.

Genetics

Some studies have shown that Narcissism can be passed down in families but whether they really do have that much influence seems to be constantly in question. Nature/Nurture/Environmental influences tend to carry more weight.

Brain Science

Whatever the cause, there is actually neuroscientific evidence their brains are different from normal people and it's worth being aware of this fact. Whether their brains are like this as a result of being narcissistic in the first place is not something I've been able to discover, but my guess, given how the brain and neuroplasticity works, is their brains are different as a result of their 'normal' or 'regular' behavior. And of course, nobody is identifying Narcissism in children to be mapping their brains at an early enough age to determine how different their brains may be from 'normal' children.

However, for adults, studies using fMRI scans have shown that there are differences in the following regions in the brain: Limbic, Hippocampus, Corpus Collosum, Amygdala and Orbitofrontal areas. Furthermore, a study in Germany found patients with NPD had less brain matter in areas that overlapped with the areas associated with empathy and compassion (i.e., left anterior insula, rostral and median cingulate cortex as well as dorsolateral and medial parts of the prefrontal cortex). When you are dealing with a narcissist, you need to remember that they are wired differently from a normal person and therefore, normal, logical, rational thinking and behavior is not something you can expect from them.

It's NOT your fault!

When you start to understand that all these factors come into play, and that NPD is a Cluster B Mental Disorder, this should make it very clear to you that it's NOT your fault. Nothing you have done, did, could have done or would do differently makes one shred of a difference to how a narcissist treats or treated you. They operate with one agenda; their own gratification above all else. Even their own children are used as pawns. They have no concern for their children's welfare and use them to meet their own utterly selfish ends. If you have been blaming yourself, as I know so many victims of narcissistic abuse do, please stop it, right now, and believe me when I say it was and is NOT your fault.

Why do they do what they do? Negative and Positive Narcissistic Supply

Narcissists need constant admiration, adoration and attention to reinforce their self-image, which is, ironically, a fake one. They are deeply unhappy, inadequate, damaged people who have no real emotions of their own, other than their pathological need for attention. They need to be the center of the Universe at all times and this attention gives them 'narcissistic supply' – also known as 'fuel', which validates them and keeps them feeling happy and in control. Fuel can be good or bad. It's all the same to them, as long as the focus is firmly on them.

Positive Supply

At the beginning of the relationship, you will be smitten, besotted and falling in love with this person, so you will be giving them bucket loads of 'fuel' which makes them happy. Because they are mirroring you, you're loving everything about them and heaping praise and compliments on them, but you don't realize what is going on. You're just caught up in the heady romantic fumes at this point. Understandably. It's intoxicating. It's easy to keep pouring positive fuel all over them because you are genuinely happy and joyful to be with them. If you only knew what was to come...

Negative Supply

The positive supply stage can last a long time, but invariably, the negative stage begins, and that's when they start devaluing you and the negative fuel comes from seeing you hurt, confused, angry, crying, depressed, raging... they don't care that you are in emotional (or physical) pain. As long as you are directing your anger, pain, etc., at them, you're giving them fuel. It's their entire reason for existing – getting that fuel from you. It's really hard to get your head around why someone could enjoy hurting another person so much, but you have to understand this is what they do, and they don't give a damn how much they hurt you along their way to ultimately destroying you.

Who is affected by NPD?

People from all walks of life, race, creed, and color, sexual orientation – are all potential targets. Your age, looks, profession, intelligence etc., are all irrelevant. What the narcissist is looking for is a specific kind of person and I will be sharing all their tricks and tactics in this book, so you will know how to protect yourself from them.

Is it only women who are affected?

I want to address this briefly because a lot of people think that it is ONLY women who are affected by evil narcissistic men, but that's not the case. It's true that statistically, far more women are abused but men suffer too. According to the DSM-5, between 0.5 and 1 percent of the general population is diagnosed with NPD and 75% are men. Which still leaves plenty room for Females.

I have a support group for men and work with guys who are trying to heal from the abuse. Female narcissists are more deadly and venomous because they have society on their side, as in, it's hard for society to believe that women can abuse men – women have traditionally been thought of as the 'weaker' or the 'gentler' sex. Men are physically stronger. It's also a social taboo or stigma for men to admit they have been abused, so it makes it very difficult for them to stand up and be counted. But it's happening all the time and probably a lot more than we realize because men are too ashamed or scared to seek help.

There are 5 reasons I've talked about regarding men being abused and I'd like to cover those here for any guys who might have picked up a copy of this book.

Female narcissists are skillful liars

They lie skillfully and make themselves look like victims. They'll twist everything you say or do to make it look like you're the villain and everyone will fall for it because they are so damned good at it. You're left reeling, knowing they've lied, but you can't prove it. The web of lies they spin leaves you feeling like you're going out of your mind. And that's exactly how they want you to feel. They enjoy their power over you.

Men are the tough ones!

Another reason is that men are supposed to be tough, so it's both difficult and incredibly demeaning to their self-esteem to have to admit that they are being emotionally and psychologically abused by a woman. This adds to the sense of isolation they feel because they can't tell anyone, for fear of looking like a complete fool. Often there is just no one they can confide in.

Female narcissists hunt kind, generous guys!

Another reason is that Narcissists of both sexes typically seek out 'victims' who they know they can manipulate. That means they are looking for a guy with a kind, gentle heart and loving, forgiving ways. The kind of guy any normal woman would love to have in her life, because they have a great capacity for love, but their giving heart very quickly becomes a stomping ground for their hateful, mentally ill narcissistic partner.

Shame begets shame

And yet another reason is that shame begets shame, and rather than stand up to their partner when she is abusive or unreasonable in public, a man will more than likely try to defend her, saying things like 'She had a terrible childhood' or 'Her Ex was really awful to her' or any other excuse that helps them to gloss over what's really going on. Because it's simply too shameful and painfully embarrassing for them to admit the truth – that they are living with an abusive partner. They are effectively hiding their own shame beneath a public façade. One may even deny the truth to oneself much of the time.

They're experts at ' ' you back up

I've lost count of the times I've heard that every time the guy says he's had enough, and he really has, he breaks up... but within a matter of days, often just hours, the Ex is back texting or calling like crazy, declaring how much she loves you, can't live without you, can't stop thinking about you, yada yada... and you fall for it. Not just once, time and time again. She's so good at convincing you that she will try to change (while passively-aggressively pointing out all your faults and blaming you, which in turn makes you start believing that you could have/should have done better) and you believe her.

So back you go and this time, she gets her hooks even deeper into you and 'love bombs' you for a few days, a few weeks maybe, before she starts her crazy-making behavior yet again. It's a vicious cycle and the only way to end it is to END it, go no contact and never let her back into your life. She won't change, because she can't. She is hard-wired to keep on hurting you because that is the only way she can validate herself. It's a toxic mentality but people who stay in a relationship like this do so because of trauma bonding. I'll cover this later in the book. Being in a relationship with a narcissist is a very complicated place to be, and even more complicated to get out of.

How widespread is NPD and abuse?

Licensed Clinical Social Worker and founder of World Narcissistic Abuse Awareness Day (WNAAD) Bree Bonchay, in an article on Psych Central, shares some fascinating number-crunching carried out by Sandra L Brown, founder of the Institute for Relational Harm Reduction and Public Pathology Education, on people who are potentially damaged by abuse caused by the 'no conscience' disorders. She bases her calculations on just 6% of the population known to have antisocial/psychopathic disorders and if those only affected 5 people each in their lives, she comes out with a staggering 3.4 billion people. That's the shocking truth - nearly half the population of the planet! And you know what, I don't think she's wrong. I already know without a doubt, your average NP Disordered person will target a far greater number of victims to feed their insatiable hunger for narcissistic supply during their lifetimes. I'll post the links to both articles in the Reading and Resources Section at the end of the book.

Because NPD is typically so insidious in nature and because narcissists don't see themselves as people who need help, I'm speculating that millions of them go undiagnosed for their whole live. Those who do go and get diagnosed do so because they have been court mandated or referred by their physician, so the real number of people who have NPD, AND those who are affected, could be far higher. It's a frightening thought. It's all the more reason to be aware of their tactics and how they operate. Romantic predators are narcissists – wolves in sheep's clothing, and this book is all about helping you how to know their tricks, and not fall into their traps. So let's start getting into the nitty-gritty of how they operate, and put the top 50 Red Flags under the microscope.

So what happens when you meet a Narcissist?

Meeting a narcissist can leave you feeling totally enchanted, to a degree that is simply beyond the comprehension of anyone who has not experienced it personally. One of the most profound descriptions I've come across of how this can feel was written by author Lee Miller, in his excellent book, 'Dating Harley Quinn: My 3 Years With A Female Narcissist'. I am grateful to Lee for giving me permission to share this with you:

"The feeling Harley Quinn gave was perfect purity of perfection. I quite literally could not imagine a girl more totally perfect; my imagination was stretched just to take in the reality of her. Her day-to-day existence was ALREADY beyond the limits of my imagination. And she was MY girlfriend. This pure, distilled, graceful, artistic, intelligent, funny, multilingual, deeply loving visage sent by the gods was my girlfriend. She took me in every way she possibly could to the heights beyond the top of Mount Everest in sensual and hedonistic pleasure - to a land where my daily life was so far beyond. Beyond the beyond that is the outer limits of human experience. A land that only movies even touch upon and no one gets to live. To the edge of the stratosphere where the air is so thin you have to wear a space suit but the view - the view is all humanity stretched out before you and you can see the curvature of the earth and the blackness of space. You know that above you, there isn't

even enough air to support your wings, there is no higher. This is it. Beyond this point there is no measurement of height, from here on it becomes - distance. As you glide in perfect tranquility at the edge of space, the sun so bright your visor is almost black, gasping at the beauty of life that you never thought possible."

Wow! Narcissists are that good!

Here's a typical scenario for your first meeting with Mr. or Ms. Overt or Covert Narcissist, out in full romantic predator regalia and whom, you will not realize at this stage, has pre-selected you using a mind-boggling array of detective tactics.

This gorgeous person approaches you. Your common sense flies out the window, for a number of reasons. But let's start with this one: they are so utterly charming, good-looking and well-turned out, that you're instantly beguiled by them and when they turn the full force of their charm on YOU, you're instantly flattered that someone so attractive could be interested in you. Who can blame you? It's intoxicating to think that someone so handsome or beautiful and sexy, finds you so alluring. You throw caution entirely to the wind.

In this exciting beginning, you ignore any signs that might be telling you that something is not quite right here, because this person is just so hot and they seem – well, just so into you! They seem to just GET you! You bury your doubts and because the nature of some narcissists is that they will very quickly get under your skin by bombarding you with gifts, fabulous nights out, compliments galore and amazing sex, you barely have time to think straight. You'll be whisked into a whirlwind of romantic proportions so epic that your head will be spinning with delight.

They will be calling you, texting you, emailing you and turning up at all hours of the day and night, at your home, your workplace or social venues that they somehow suddenly know you frequent.

You might wonder why or how they know you work here, or drink with friends there or like this particular restaurant, but because they are so good at manipulation, lies and subterfuge, they'll come up with plausible lies that will slip off their tongues like quicksilver on glass. And again, because you're so caught up in the whirlwind of attraction, you'll ignore all the warning signs.

The truth is they are hiding in VERY plain sight, if you could just step back and see what's going on. The fact is, in the brief intro that I've written above, there are 7 blatant Red Flags that you could have picked up on within days, if not hours, of meeting a narcissist for the first time. I'm going to cover all of them and give you some solid tips on what to do instead of going gaga! I'll then go into the rest of the Top 50 (but there are more out there!) so by the end of this book, you'll be well informed about what to look for and how to easily spot a narcissist and avoid the traps. If you know what to look for, you can save yourself from the nightmare of narcissistic abuse. You can save yourself from YEARS of heartache. So let's get started!

CHAPTER TWO

THE TOP 50 RED FLAGS OF THE ROMANTIC PREDATOR – aka THE NARCISSIST

'If more people became skilled at identifying a narcissist at the seduction stage, then more people would avoid the abuse that occurs during devaluation and the emotional confusion and trauma that arises from the discard.'

'The cost to those who get sucked into the tornado that is the narcissist is substantial and more people ought to be warned and understand how to spot the narcissist '.
Both quotes from 'Ultra Elite' narcissist, HG Tudor

'I never missed one red flag. I saw each one fall and chose to look the other way. I loved you more than anything, including myself. And therein lies the lesson. I learned it so goddamn hard.'
Author Unknown

I'm going to break the Red Flags down into stages, because typically these are the stages you'll have to go through in the life cycle of a narcissistic relationship.

So, I'm going to kick off at the start, the 'Initial Meeting/Early Days', I'll then look at 'Getting Deeper into the Relationship', because if you've chosen to ignore the warning signs and plunged ahead you'll need to know these Flags. Don't feel bad if this happened to you, because it happens to everyone who gets targeted by a narcissist. Remember they are experts at what they do and this book is designed to help you to never fall into their trap again.

Then I will cover the BIG Red Flags of Narcissistic Abuse. I regularly receive messages from people who say they didn't even realize they were in an abusive relationship until they Googled something along the lines of 'Why is my husband always angry with me' or a friend sent them a link to my group and they came to learn about NPD and abuse for the first time. 'OMG', a woman recently wrote to me, 'Have you been the fly on the wall in my marriage? What you've described is exactly what has been happening to me! I'm being abused by a narcissist!'

Narcissistic behavior during this final stage is typical and predictable, but so are the resultant symptoms of the abuse, so knowing what to expect if you're in a relationship will help you to determine if you are dealing with a narcissist and if you are, you have to get out and stay out. The abuse is horrendous and if you don't get out, it's going to happen to you. If it's happening already, please reach out and get help. I'll put links to mine and other resources at the end of the book. So, let's dive in and get familiar with the Top 50 Red Flags of Romantic Predators.

INITIAL MEETING/EARLY DAYS
Red Flag Nos 1 to 26

Red Flag No 1: Not trusting your intuition!

This is by far the biggest Red Flag of all, because if you had just trusted your gut from the outset, you'd never have allowed yourself to get sucked in in the first place. I've lost count of the people who've told me that they knew, they just *knew* something was off, but they ignored the warning signs and alarm bells. If you're reading this now, in the wake of your own narcissistic relationship, I'm betting you'll be nodding your head in agreement. But why? Why did you not heed the warning signs? Because romantic predatory narcissists are slick, seductive, often sexy and deadly. Or at least, the covert malignant ones are and the overts very often are too. One woman who commented on a post about ignoring Red Flags in Facebook said:

'I ignored the Red Flags because the good was SO GOOD!'

Even if you don't fancy the pants off them, they can still overpower you, as another woman shared with me:

"It's funny as I never fancied my first Narc. At first, I gave him 2 out of 10, but I fell in love with being swept off my feet."

So, you brush it aside, even the obvious flaws, or you consider the little quirks in their behavior as not so important or even persuade yourself that you imagined it. Because the good is just so good and you don't want to cast any shadows of doubt on this beautiful new relationship. And that good can be just about YOU feeling good about yourself, and NOT about how you feel about the predator. That's an interesting thing to think about isn't it?

What is happening here is that you're getting a blast of self-love, something that is missing in your life and you perhaps don't even realize it. If you know anything about my work, you'll be aware that I am always bringing it back to self-love and self-worth because these are absolutely critical in this whole sorry saga of narcissistic abuse. I've learned from years of working with people to help them heal from various forms of traumatic abuse that self-love, self-esteem and self-image are closely connected with being vulnerable to attracting multiple abusers.

But back to the now and all that beautiful good which turns very ugly – whether you're head over heels in love with this new person or whether you've fallen in love with yourself - you will live to very deeply regret not trusting yourself. I've also heard it said, way too often...

'Looking back, I remember thinking 'Wow! He seems too good to be true!' I wish I had listened to my gut.'

If they seem too good to be true, they almost certainly are. That is actually another big Red Flag all by itself because most of them DO seem too good to be true. They are so good at their own brand of seduction, even when you don't feel attracted to them, they can still hook you.

But what if I CAN'T trust my intuition?

This applies if you've been in a narcissistic relationship and are ready to get back into the dating scene, or you *have a desire to* because you want to be in a loving relationship, but you are paralyzed by the fear of walking into another narcissist 's trap. You've been so badly betrayed, deceived and hurt and you just don't trust your own instincts any more. I've heard so many people say this and I understand why it happens. It's part of a protective or defense mechanism to keep us safe from more harm, but it can literally make you paranoid and in the early stages of wanting to find a new partner, you will suspect everyone of being a narcissist.

Or, you will be so disillusioned by what has happen to you that you'll swear to never get into another relationship again. This is also common and makes total sense, because if you burned your finger on the cooker, you'd be a lot more careful next time you were near the cooker. If you'd left a job because you hated the work, you wouldn't go out looking for another job exactly the same. When we've been hurt by something or someone, we seek to avoid situations where we might get hurt again.

And the Vulnerable Narcissists? They reel you in emotionally just as fast

Not all narcissists are showy, gorgeous or sexy, as I think is clear from the 'Types' I've outlined earlier on. The 'Vulnerable' narcissist is just as deadly. They may be average looking (or even unattractive to you) but they still have the power to reel you in. They present differently, have a knack for making you feel sorry for them, wanting to help heal them, or mother them. They have a way of getting under your sympathetic or empathetic skin.

Very often, they're not sexually motivated at all, but they'll convince you it's because they are nervous, shy, or inexperienced and you'll feel challenged to be the one who changes all that. In reality, they are often asexual and don't want to have anything to do with sex, so even if you do succeed a few times in the early stages, sex will soon be off the menu.

You actually need to be even more aware of this type because they are working on your emotional buttons and using their manipulative skills to fool you into thinking that they are so sweet, kind, misunderstood, the product of a horrible childhood and so on, and your kind, empathetic nature allows you to fall for it. Even though initially you don't even fancy them, you end up hooked because they've created a bond with you and convinced you that nobody understands them like you do. You feel needed and appreciated like never before. You'll walk on water for a while, until you are plunged into the deep murky waters of narcissistic abuse.

The abuse from this type of narcissist is often very subtle, passive-aggressive and leaves you feeling inferior and worthless, and you don't even know why. I've had clients say things to me like:

'I don't understand why I feel like this. My partner is never abusive. He's never hit me or anything like that. But somehow, I just always feel that I am beneath him. I can't put my finger on it. I feel like I'm just not good enough for him.'

When I start digging with clients, by asking them a lot of questions, the light bulbs start popping as they realize that they are being victimized by a covert, vulnerable narcissist. And it really hurts to realize that you've been abused in this way. So, watch out for the quiet ones. They are silent and deadly.

These types might also tell you they are no good for you, they will cause you pain, or you'll regret getting involved with them. They won't say this in a threatening way, oh no, they'll play this by saying something like, 'I'm not the easiest person to love' and this is a subtle challenge that taps into your emotions too. You want to be the person to change all that. If you ever hear this kind of talk from a potential partner, BELIEVE them. It's a Red Flag in itself.

How to avoid the trap - my advice

Tune in and ask yourself WHY are you feeling uneasy? All your life, you've been learning about people. We all do it, from the time we're born, and start picking up signals from our parents and other influential people in our lives, right on up to the current moment. Even if you've been abused and grew up with narcissistic parents, there is still that internal radar warning you. I well understand how growing up in such an environment distorts your worldview and why you then attract more narcissists into your life, but it doesn't change this fact: how we FEEL around people is important. If you feel something is wrong, or off, or odd, or even vaguely *familiar* about this new suitor, tune in carefully and ask yourself: What is it about them that's causing this feeling?

Something they've said or done has not sat right with you, but because the 'good is so good', you're inclined to brush it aside. Don't do this! Honor your inner voice because it will save you from a ton of heartbreak down the line. Read this book a couple of times so that you're on Red Alert about the potential Red Flags. Highlight the ones that resonate most with you, and dig deep and ask yourself what is it you need to learn about yourself here? And keep watching and listening carefully to this person's words, actions and see how often the emotional alarm bells ring for you. If they start piling up, then bring the potential relationship to a swift end.

Expect that person to start pleading with you to give them a second chance or whatever. If they do this, it's another Red Flag. Block them and move on. There is a perfectly good, decent someone out there waiting to meet you. You do not need to grasp at the artificial carrots a narcissist will dangle in front of you in the form of flowery words, declarations of love (that come way too soon) expensive gifts, trips or anything else that seems too good to be true. Remember that if it *does seem* too good to be true, it probably is. Value and respect yourself enough to know that you do not need validation from anyone else to justify who you are, how attractive, smart or good you are. You only need that validation from yourself.

They may be 'Altruistic' narcissists… two words that really don't belong in the same sentence. These are the ones who are wealthy and use their wealth to paint themselves as generous, philanthropic angels, giving large sums to charities and good causes, buying lots of gifts for people and generally making everyone think they are wonderful people. You'll be drawn in very easily when money is being thrown around like confetti at a wedding and you're on the receiving end. This is when it's so important to remember that old saying: 'All that glitters is not gold'. Try not to ignore the warning signs again.

They can also be poor but appear altruistic by constantly showing up to do charity work, volunteering at the church and so on, where they will be seen by others as being kind and caring but it's always a façade. It's part of their plan of showing their fake person to the public, but you get to see the real person behind the mask, behind closed doors.

Trusting your intuition again is something that can take time, but one of the important things to do is think back to when you met your Ex. Did you feel warnings that you ignored? If you did, your intuition was intact then and it can be again. And this time you will know to listen to it.

And realize the value this book has in helping you to KNOW what to look for. You don't have to rely on your gut alone. You can learn the tricks of the narcissist's trade and be switched on to them. Remember good old common sense? You still have that, you just misplaced it for a while too, but as you start tuning back into yourself, these natural abilities will come back.

If you feel like you don't want to date ever again, that's understandable but give yourself some time to get over and heal, from the abuse. Then re-evaluate where you are and how you feel about being alone for the rest of your life. If you feel that this is the right way forward for you, that's fine, there's absolutely nothing wrong with being alone. But if you really would love to be in a loving, trusting, fulfilling relationship, don't give up on love. Do not allow the narcissist to win. They have taken enough from you; don't let them take your future happiness.

Red Flag No 2: Judging a book by its cover

The Covert Narcissist /The Overt Narcissist

Ok so Mr. or Ms. Covert or Overt Narcissist is drop-dead gorgeous! They look like a million dollars, are in great shape, and you're almost drooling at the sight of them. When they start talking to you - via a method they have already carefully engineered, such as bumping into you or spilling a drink over you by 'accident' – of which you'll be blissfully unaware – you'll be blinded by the vision of gorgeousness in front of you. You've already started to ALLOW yourself to get hooked because you're looking at the purely superficial.

But you've just experienced your first 'Narc Attack' I can't help but mention here how well that rhymes with 'Shark Attack' and there are parallels that can be drawn. Sharks are predators who stalk their prey once they have tracked it down. They will often take a bite out of it to see if it's going to be the tasty meal they are looking for before moving in for the kill. A narcissist will do something very similar, by gauging your reaction when they first meet you. Usually they will know how you are going to react (because of their research, which I'll be covering later) but they are always testing the waters, and just like the shark, testing what is floating in the waters.

However, at this point, you'll be blissfully unaware of this. You're still too caught up in this gorgeous person in front of you. And what's even more amazing is... they're not with an equally gorgeous person. They're alone! Could this be your lucky day or could it be the unluckiest day of your life? Well, if you judge a book by its cover, then yes it could be your unluckiest. You can't possibly know that this person is a viper in Armani or Chanel. This leads me nicely into how to avoid the trap.

How to avoid the trap - my advice

That old saying about the book cover has huge merit, because you absolutely cannot judge any person's character by their outward appearance. They could be dressed in rags but have the kindest heart you've ever encountered. When you spot a gorgeous person who then hones in on you, feel flattered by all means but keep your cynical guard up. Ask yourself what is this person really like underneath? Ask yourself why is this person alone? (See Red Flag No 10, below for more on this.)

Admire how they look but keep it to yourself. Narcissists usually look good and expect compliments. Buck their trend and resist the temptation to tell them they look amazing, fabulous or whatever might be going through your head. Keep it to yourself. This type of narcissist is used to using his or her power to wow their prey. By denying them the instant gratification they are used to getting, you're also sending a signal that you're not an easy target.

BE WARNED! In this case, you can also be seen as a powerful challenge that the narcissist needs to win, so they can switch into overdrive and work very hard indeed to capture your heart. If you try to slow things down, they can become even more persistent. That's another Red Flag. Why does someone who doesn't know you AT ALL want you so desperately? Don't let your ego run away with you; keep your cool and don't fall for it.

The Vulnerable aka Introverted or Shy Narcissist

The same applies to the vulnerable narcissist. Just because they seem so, doesn't make them so. You need to tread very carefully to detect these types, but some big Red Flags to look out for are excessive 'neediness', wanting to be with you all the time, making it seem like they can't function without you, hyper-sensitive, self-absorbed, victim mentality (poor me!) and emotionally immature. Actually, several of those apply to all narcissists but with the shy ones, it often comes off as endearing that they 'need' you so much and that triggers your nurturing, caring, empathetic nature. You want to take care of them, love them and help them.

How to avoid the trap - my advice

STOP, the minute you find yourself feeling like this. If they are endearing in their neediness, ask yourself: do you really want a relationship with someone who needs mothering? Do you want someone who is going to be desperately clingy and jealous? Or do you want someone who is confident, self-assured and comfortable in his or her own skin? Consider this carefully and ask yourself why you feel drawn to help this person?

The narcissistic dance of deception can only be played out if there are two to tango. What is going on in you that makes you want to be the caregiver here? How much has this got to do with YOUR OWN need to be needed? Or to be loved? What has happened in your life to make you feel this way? You need to dig deep on this and do some self-analysis and soul-searching. Become your own therapist or seek the help of a professional if you have a history of abuse and attracting toxic people into your life. The answers lie within YOU.

Remind yourself of this fact: Further down the line in the relationship with a vulnerable narcissist , you can expect huge doses of passive-aggressive behavior. You can expect to be slowly and systematically undermined, devalued and the self that you were will shrivel and curl up into a ball of anxiety, wrapped in a heavy cloak of worthlessness. Mr. or Ms. Vulnerable will already be with their next target.

I just want to digress for a minute here – I dislike using that word 'target' to describe a human being, but when we're talking about narcissists, unfortunately to them that's just what you are. They are just like the hunter who goes out seeking targets to shoot. The narcissist is looking for the next target to ensnare in his/her trap. It's not pretty but it's the truth. To them you are nothing more than that – and bizarrely, it's NOT personal. To them anyway.

It IS personal to you however, because they've come into your life and turned it upside down, but it has nothing to do with who you are. That's a tough one to get your head around, I know. You need to realize that you are not to blame here. It wasn't something you said, didn't say, did, didn't do, could have, should have or would have done... nothing you could have said or done differently would have made any difference. Because you can't please a narcissist. When they get past the 'Love Bombing' stage and enter the devaluing one, they thrive on strife, chaos and your pain. That's what makes them happy. NPD is a very sick, pathological disorder.

Red Flag No 3: Powerful sexual attraction

Sex is a big issue for many narcissists, particularly if they are somatic narcissists. This is more so because they know it's a powerful method of attraction that creates addiction and quickly ensnares you. Sex is also a way to create emotional connections and this works well for both men and women. Women who are not narcissists tend to find more of an emotional connection with their partners than men do when it comes to sex. Not always, but in the majority of cases, they do.

Female narcissists, on the other hand know that men generally enjoy sex and they use that knowledge and their considerable sexual magnetism, to get their guy into bed as quickly as possible and provide amazing sex, thus securing their target's desire for more of the same, ASAP. When the guy has fallen hook, line and sinker for the female narcissist, the sexual/emotional connection is all the more powerful.

However, the female narcissist is not comfortable AT ALL with intimacy, but she's fantastic at PRETENDING GOOD SEX. She'll give you the best sex of your life and it'll blow your mind. This is an incredibly powerful weapon because great sex makes you feel great. Your emotions and 'love chemicals' are firing on all cylinders and you're thinking, how can sex be this good if she's not wildly attracted to and crazy in love with you? You know good sex when you get it and this IS IT! But, it's not; it's all an act that she's putting on to make you feel that way. It's a potent weapon that leaves you powerless in its wake.

The stronger the sexual attraction, the more difficult this is to ignore because sexual desire creates an intoxicating rush of chemicals that are suddenly rocketing around your body – testosterone, estrogen, dopamine, serotonin, oxytocin – all powerful seductive manipulators themselves. It's called sexual chemistry for a reason!

When a very good-looking narcissist applies this technique, your brain is getting excited by lust, desire, attraction and the anticipation of things to come. It's an extremely potent weapon in the hands of a narcissist. They can also be sexually forceful, putting pressure on you to have sex with them under the guise of 'Wanting you so badly they can't think straight'. Uh oh! Watch out!

How to avoid the trap - my advice

This is a tough one, because your brain has kicked into overdrive and you're not thinking clearly. But you need to step back and give yourself a good talking to. You're fiercely attracted to this person but you don't KNOW them. You don't know the dangers that could be lurking inside them (and there is also the danger of STDs and pregnancy, if you do decide to throw caution to the wind and have unsafe sex – something they will also often push you into) and if they are indeed a narcissist, you're letting yourself in for heartache that is never, ever going to be worth it. You'll pay in blood, sweat, tears, a broken heart, emotional battery and financial destruction. Step back, take your time and get to know them first. Don't get caught up in their whirlwind of fake flattery and sexual attraction.

Ground yourself in reality. The following are a few tips on how to do that!

Tip No 1

If you're feeling the throttle of sexual desire, take yourself away from the person for a few minutes of privacy. Go to the bathroom or wherever you can and take a few deep breaths and remind yourself that you are doing this to protect yourself from a potential romantic predator narcissist! If you've had the misfortune of being in a previous narcissistic relationship, recall the early days with that person, remember the warning bells you chose to ignore. Decide that this time, you are not going to ignore them. Decide that this time, no sex on the planet could ever be worth going through that hell again.

Then go back. Cool, calm and collected. Observe how they behave when you return. Do they try to pick up where they left off, hitting you up with sexual innuendo or even blatant comments? They might say things like 'I want you right here, right now', even if it's in the middle of a busy bar. Or 'I could F*** you right now and it would blow my mind!' If they are capable of saying these kinds of things in public, imagine how steamy it would get if they got you alone. This kind of approach is designed to keep pushing your sexual desire buttons. Don't fall for it. Tell them that you think they are attractive (stoke their ego a BIT – don't overdo it), but you really don't like to rush things. If they keep pushing and gushing about how desirable you are and how they want you so badly, picture that massive Red Flag blowing in the winds all around you. Then leave them.

Tip No 2

Nothing muddies the water faster than sex early on in a relationship! Sex creates an emotional intimacy by the very nature of the act. It's also great at distancing you from reality and when you're trying to be clear-headed in determining if this person is a narcissist, sex isn't going to help you to do that. So, don't have sex with them on the first, second, third, fourth or fifth dates. I know, I said it was going to be tough, but what you're doing here is trying to figure out if this person is a narcissist, right? You're not trying to get laid as fast as you can. Observe their behavior and note if they are always trying to engage you sexually. When you kiss them goodnight, do they want to take it to the next level immediately?

Stop, and think. Why is this person's sexuality so domineering? Could they have an end game, a hidden agenda? Back up and give yourself space and by the time this happens, you should be adding up the Red Flags as you go along and if you're seeing several, do not get into bed with this person. You will LONG regret it. Trust me!

But what if it's too late, and you've already slept with them?

Ok, so let's say you got to this book too late, or even, you've read the warning flag but you still couldn't resist and you had sex on the first date or so. Does that mean that you are now doomed forever? No, it doesn't. Maybe at this point there weren't enough flags showing up for you to really believe that this person – this utterly gorgeous person – could be evil deep down. I understand, and I'll remind you how good they are at this romantic seduction game. They're VERY good at it. What you need to do now is watch very carefully for their behavior and Red Flag No 4 is going to help you with what to look out for. If you are dealing with a narcissist you've just had sex with, you are going to be subjected to most, if not all, of these flags.

Tip No 3

Avoid alcohol because we all know that alcohol consumption lowers your resistance and in these situations, it will make you much more likely to share more than just your body, and if you end up drinking way too much, you'll probably forget a lot of what you've shared – but the Romantic Predator won't have - so make it a rule to NOT drink alcohol or keep it to a bare minimum of one or two glasses of wine or beer in those early dating days.

Red Flag No 4: – Please, for the love of God, don't fall for it!

Idealization or love bombing as it's commonly called, is an umbrella term that most people I've come across who've had to deal with a Romantic Predator have been subjected to. It's Narcissism Tactic No 1.

Normal 'flirting' is nice, but there's a big difference between flirting and Love Bombing. love bombing is totally over the top, whereas flirting is much more subtle. A look here, a light touch there and a sense that this person finds you attractive, are all part of courting rituals that have gone on forever between potential lovers and a text or two (not 200!) after a date is usually expected. It's NORMAL and you'll see me repeatedly point out in this book that Romantic Predators do not behave NORMALLY.

Now, within the love bombing stage, there are plenty of 'Flags within Flags' that you need to be aware of, as they will probably all show up and you need to be adding them up as you go along and remember that your mission is to determine if this person is a narcissist and protect yourself from the horrors a subsequent relationship would entail. It's quite possible for you to avoid and elude the narcissist very quickly when you're alert to these love bombing flags, so I want to point them all out so they are crystal clear to you. I'll refer to them as A, B, C, etc.

love bombing Flag No A: Idealization

As soon as you meet, it could even be the very FIRST time - this person will literally bombard you with compliments and declarations of love. They've never met anyone like you. You're like sunshine on a rainy day. You're balm to a painful wound. You are the woman/man they have always dreamed of. You are everything they have ever wanted. You are divine. You walk on water. This utterly over-the-top carrying on is officially known as 'Idealization' because one of the characteristic traits of NPD from the DSM-5 is:

'Is preoccupied with fantasies of unlimited success, power, brilliance, beauty or ideal love.'

The narcissist is idealizing you, thinking that maybe you are going to be the person to finally fulfill all their dreams. But their dreams are a highly unrealistic illusion, just as they themselves are a highly unrealistic illusion of a person. They are putting you on a pedestal of their own making, and turning you into a fantasy that doesn't exist.

They are doing this for several reasons that I've come to understand.

1. Because they are deluded by the 'fairy tale' romance they're holding in their heads and that vision of 'ideal love' is driving them
2. To hook you and get you to fall in love with them
3. To keep your attention firmly focused on them
4. They want to make you feel so good that you quickly become addicted to these compliments and flattery
5. Ultimately, to control you and having you head-over-heels in love with them makes their task much easier
6. To keep getting narcissistic supply

What you have to be aware of at this early stage is that none of this is real. What you are seeing is their fake self or persona. They have no real identity of their own. They 'Mirror' you and everything you do and say, to create this powerful bond. But their agenda is always on the ultimate goal, points 5 and 6 above. It's always about control and narcissistic supply.

Cognitive Empathy

It is important to understand what this is if you're not familiar with it because, as I mentioned earlier, the narcissist is able to 'fake empathy'. They are very skilled at observing, mirroring and matching the person in front of them. They will do this with words, body language and by closely observing how you behave. They can quickly learn how to mimic you in a very subtle way but this creates a strong feeling of connection with them. They learn how to behave by observing others and when they have their targets in sight, they focus wholeheartedly on this person, which often gives the target the feeling that they are the only two people in the room. Establishing this dynamic connection draws you in, and they are one step closer to getting inside your head. Effectively, they have emotionally manipulated you and you don't even know it.

If you are very careful and observant, you might notice that sometimes you say something and there is a blank look on their faces, or a flicker of doubt or confusion in their eyes, because perhaps you have said something that they don't have an immediate response for, but they will very quickly cover their tracks and mimic or mirror what you have said or done. This usually happens so fast you'll barely notice, yet when you look back, you might recall such incidences. Be on the lookout for such subtle slip-ups.

What is also interesting is that research has found that the human brain reacts differently when either cognitive or emotional empathy is activated and as you might have guessed, emotional empathy is stronger. Narcissists do not have emotional empathy.

How to avoid the trap – my advice

Ask yourself if this kind of behavior is normal? Really ask yourself and listen to your gut! Nobody falls in love and declares it on the first or second date. It's absurd. How can this person love you when they don't KNOW you? Consider all the seeming 'synchronicities' they're dropping into the conversation as highly suspect.

Take all this false flowery, fake flattery the next time you hear it... and ask yourself 'Is this genuine or could it be fake?' One of the easiest ways to determine if it IS fake is if there is just too much of it. As I said, compliments are nice and when you meet a potential new partner, it's great to get some compliments on how you look or some aspect of your personality, but a constant flow of this needs to be seen as a potential Red Flag. And think FFF... False Flowery Flattery. Run that in your head and keep your feet firmly on the ground and your head out of the clouds if you have the slightest inclination this person is going over the top in the compliments department.

Ask yourself do these compliments sound 'cookie cutter' to you? Narcissists are very predictable in their seduction techniques and they use the same phrases and tactics over and over again. You have to be cynical and I know that goes against your nature if you're an Empath, but you must do it. You have to be smarter by a mile than the narcissist because you have everything to lose, and they have nothing to lose.

love bombing Flag No B: Bombarding you with text messages

When you're apart, your phone will be on fire with messages of love, links to songs (see Flag no 6) romantic memes, poems, sexting and anything else that you might have mentioned. You'll get copious texts telling you they can't stop thinking of you. They're going out of their mind with longing for you. They've never felt this way about anyone before.

These messages will start early and go on all day and into the night, regardless of whether they know you are busy with work, kids, shopping or whatever. They are doing this to keep your mind and attention on them and they know it makes you feel SO good. They'll call you late at night, even though they know you have to be up early for work the next morning and they'll keep you on the phone for hours, waxing syrupy lyrical about how much you mean to them. And you'll lie there, tired but blissfully lapping it all up.

This is part of their underhanded agenda to get you hooked because in a very short time, you'll be so looking forward to the next message or phone call, you'll keep checking your phone and smiling and feeling good when you see more gorgeous messages of how besotted this person is with you and how wonderful you are... but then they will stop sending them. And the late-night call you've started looking forward to doesn't come. You'll start wondering what's happened... where are they? What have you done wrong? And this is where their game of abuse begins, although in reality, it began the moment they met you.

If you've slept with them early on the texts will be sizzling with how amazing the sex was or how they've never had sex like it, or how hot you were in bed and how they can't wait to make love to you again. If the sex was indeed fantastic (as it often is in the beginning, with the exception of the vulnerable narcissist) this is going to have you longing to see them and get it on again and your brain chemicals will be firing up in anticipation. More on this brain chemistry later. But see Red Flag No 34 if you want to check it out now.

How to avoid the trap – my advice

If you were not so blinded by love, desire or just being awash in all this attention, you'd be able to step back and see this for what it is: Obsessive. This is not normal behavior. Normal people do NOT do this. Give your ego a massive kick up the butt and wake up! Shake off the fairytale glitter and ask the magic question: Who does this?

If this starts happening as soon as you've met, you're already in 'Narcland.' Send one message and say sorry, bye. And block this person immediately from everywhere. If you don't do this immediately, and you're dealing with any but the vulnerable narcissist , you could fire up the narcissist 's hunting skills to the max - once the shark tastes blood, it's game over for their prey - and they will go all out to get you back. They can't resist the challenge and will do everything in their power to win you over. There is also the issue of their massive egos and injured pride. If you've dumped them before they've had a chance to dump you, this is an insult to them. They may just shrug it off and move on to the next target, but they may not. And in this case, you could already be in trouble. If you let them back in at this stage, you are in for more psychological, emotional and possibly other (physical, sexual, financial) damage, than you could possibly imagine.

If they know where you work or live, be prepared for them to show up and take evasive action if you possibly can. Leave work by a different door. Get a cab to collect you from work and take you to a friend's house. Check who's at your front door before you answer. If they refuse to back off, you may have to threaten them with calling the police, or getting a protection order. This happens more often than you would think, and I've known women who've had to do this after only a few dates.

love bombing Flag No C: Social Media Dominance

If you've connected on social media (SM), you'll likely see that this person has spent plenty of time visiting your pages. They will have liked everything, commented on everything and littered every photo of you with complimentary comments and hearts. They will also make it clear that you're now their BF/GF, that you guys are an item and they'll likely send friend requests to lots of your friends. If so, you should be very worried.

How to avoid the trap - my advice

It's very difficult to avoid connecting with people in SM these days, but in this case, try not to connect with them. Check all your FB and other social sites and go over your security and privacy settings so only your friends can see your posts. This gives you control over who you add and who sees what. Unfortunately, the Internet provides an abundant source of unsuspecting victims for Romantic Predators so you need to protect yourself as much as you can.

This has the double advantage of making it more difficult for a potential predator to find out more about you during their 'research' stage and it prevents them from requesting to become friends. They will undoubtedly ask you to connect with them. You're going to have to steel yourself and tell them you don't want to connect at this time. If they are pushing (ladling on the charm as they do), visualize a HUGE RED FLAG waving in the wind, and don't give in. A normal person will NOT be desperate to connect with you on SM.

If you've let them in and they've connected with several of your friends, what you need to realize is that they are very likely going to do any or all of these things:

1. Groom/charm your friends surreptitiously as potential supply
2. Charm them into finding out more about you to use against you later
3. Groom them as potential 'flying monkeys' (Red Flag No 46) to use against you when the inevitable discard happens

I am hearing and seeing examples of this every day in my groups. This is what they are up to ALL the time. You might also suddenly find that several of their friends have requested to be friends with you and of course in your excitement and delight that they were told about you, you'll accept them. If they are in already, get them out. Unfriend and block them. They are only there to do more damage to you in the long run. There's a ton more that I could say about Facebook – having to close your account, protect yourself from their fake FB Profiles and so on (it's ridiculously easy to create a fake profile!), but I'll just remind you it's a wise move to clean up your security/friends lists and don't let anyone in who you don't trust with your life.

love bombing Flag No D: They shower you with compliments

Most people enjoy a compliment here and there, but when you're with a Romantic Predator they come at you thick and fast. They compliment you about everything, and tell you you're looking amazing, even when you're totally not and you know it. You might think they are being sweet and how wonderful it is that they love you even when you look a mess... but these are false compliments and you must, at the very least, take them with a pinch of salt.

How to avoid the trap – my advice

Put your ego to the side. Declare to yourself that wow, yes, isn't it nice to have someone going this nuts over me, then stop and give yourself a reality check. Step back, emotionally, from this person. And ask yourself, could this person be a fake? Could they just be trying to trap me? Am I in the sights of a freakin' narcissist? And keep asking yourself questions. What's so fabulous about me all of a sudden? Why is this person going so overboard? Isn't this behavior a bit over the top (OTT)?

It's hard to stop a person who's hell-bent on paying you every compliment under the sun, so just accept them at this point. Don't ask any questions outright. Very often, when a narcissist does this, they are automatically expecting you to reply in kind and that gives them fuel. Don't do it. Remember, narcissists crave admiration, adoration, attention – they NEED it. Giving it to them at the outset tells them that you're a hot target for them. Resist, with all of your might, the temptation to tell them how wonderful they are. If you can do this and resist their attempts, the narcissist will realize that you are not the soft target that they thought you were.

They might lose interest in you at this point and that, frankly, would be a blessing for you, but you'll only know that when you know it was a potential narcissist. And I'll just add a reminder here of the warning I mentioned earlier: it might also cause them to see you as a bigger challenge that must be won over. So, you've got to be even more on your guard.

love bombing Flag No E: Showing up every which way

In addition to all the other flags, they'll 'surprise' you by turning up unexpectedly at all times of the day and night, to your home or place of work as soon as they learn both locations. They'll tell you that they couldn't stop thinking about you, had to see you, are going crazy missing you – even if it's only been a very short while and you let yourself believe it because it feels so damned good to be desired like this. It's hard to get your head out of the clouds if you're deeply attracted to this person, but you have to for your sanity's sake. If you don't, you'll live to regret it.

When someone you've just met starts behaving like this, you have to step back and realize what you already know. **This is NOT normal.** Nobody falls head-over-heels in love this fast. Yes, you might see someone across a crowded room and think that they are the one you're going to marry, but you then spend time getting to know them and you could well end up with them. But if they are exhibiting all the usual narcissistic Red Flags, you should be tallying these up in your mind as a means to protect yourself from getting totally sucked in.

Now you have 6 love bombing Red Flags. All of this OTT behavior is designed to have you fall in love and become obsessed with this person in record time. It's aimed at getting you addicted to them and by being in your world every way they can in these early stages, they are giving you little time to think of anything BUT them. It's as if you've shot up on heroin and all you can think of is your next fix and it comes fast, but you want more. You can't get enough of it and the narcissist knows this. You are falling so fast, you can't even begin to contemplate how any of this could go wrong.

How could you, when you don't know what you are dealing with? You only know when it's too late and this monstrous person has emotionally and psychologically brutalized you. The narcissist is getting a ton of positive fuel from you at this time because of course you're reciprocating with love, compliments, adoration for them and that will keep them happy for a time. How much time? It depends but one thing is for sure... this 'honeymoon' period is not going to last.

If you're encountering a combination of these Red Flags in the first few dates, my advice to you is this: get the hell out of Dodge because it's full of smoking guns and the bullets are all heading for you!

love bombing Flag No F: Music and Me!

Music is one of the most powerful tools in the Romantic Predator's arsenal. Let's face it, there are so many great songs out there and the vast majority of them are about love. The narcissist will very quickly learn the kind of music you're into, and they will waste no time in using the songs you love to convey their love to you.

They'll send song links to your phone, they'll hum or whistle the tune when they are with you (often making it look like they don't realize you're listening, but trust me, they know), they'll make playlists of all the songs they know you love and put them on a flash drive or send you a Spotify link. They will gift this to you with a syrupy message of love. They will quickly identify 'Our Song' and make sure they have it in their car, in their home (if you get to visit them there) or your home, they'll change their ring tone to your song and it will haunt you for the rest of your life. Because that's one of the reasons they do it. They want to create a bond that will be impossible for you to break. Even after they have devalued and discarded you, the moment you hear that song, you'll crumble into pieces because of the poignant, beautiful memories it evokes. And they know this. They deliberately set it up to be this way.

Triggers like these will plague you but take heart, if you're in a pit of despair right now. There is a way out and you absolutely can heal from this abuse. I work with people all the time to help them break the bonds and will share more on this later.

How to avoid the trap: My advice

The only thing you can do here is to downplay your love of music. Don't react when you hear your favorite song or artist and you're with this potential predator. Be non-reactive. If they know you do love this song (they will have researched you on SM and will have seen your posts – Red Flag No 6 will clarify this) and they mention the song – take this as another big Red Flag. They do this to get your response. They'll be expecting you to confirm that wow, yes, you LOVE this song. Don't do this. Instead, say something bland like 'Yeah, it's ok.' And move on. This might throw them off because they were sure they were on the right track, but they can't say anything can they? Keep your music preferences to yourself. Don't let there be an 'Our Song' at this stage in the relationship. Save that for when you know you are on solid ground with a real person.

Here are just a few examples from people who've kindly shared their experience of love bombing (and various other tactics that I'll be discussing in this book) with me:

- *Talking badly about everyone he knew the night we met but constantly praising me*

- *Wanting to be in my company 24/7 claiming he hated to be away from me*

- *Staring into my eyes for long periods of time as though he was love struck*

- *The 'crazy' look that would appear on his face when questioned about something that didn't add up, dark eyes and the anger outbursts*

- *Hamster wheel conversations that move in circles having no resolution that you just end because you grow so tired*

- *Turning up outside my work when my shift is over like every day he could, to walk me home. I thought this was so sweet but would run a mile if it happened again*

- *Kept me talking on the phone constantly – that's if he wasn't constantly texting - and very long paragraphs too!!!*

- *Asking me to expensive restaurants then "forgetting" his wallet*

- *Making a fake dating profile of a guy who likes every single thing I liked...like from heaven, the perfect guy...I knew it was him...so I asked the fake profile the same questions I'd texted my ex...finally got him caught up and he did admit. Wish I kept that text for court.*

- *Falling in love too fast. Alcohol or drug dependency. Blame. Criticizing. Finding weaknesses and using them against you.*

- *Constantly keeping tabs on me*

- *Writing checks his ass couldn't cash!*

- Promises and disappointment ALL THE TIME

- Needing complete control over any conversation

- Rudely interrupting and carrying on

- Throwing hissy-fit attitudes over petty things

- Mine made me think he was wealthy. Our entire marriage existed on debt

- If you say "no" and they take it as a personal offense

- If you make a comment that they disagree with, they go crazy. CRAZY!!!

- Making friends uncomfortable so that they tend to keep their distance, they don't want the drama

- Feel like a child getting in trouble if you don't answer your phone or get something they want done

- Wanting to know where you are every moment of the day yet dare you wonder where they are! Do as I say not as I do!

- Early Love Bombing, demand for physical attention, wanted everything too soon

- Had a string of grieving women he not only told me about but laughed about

- He was soooo charming and good looking and he knew it. What would I do differently? I would not have laughed at his stupid jokes. Told him no thanks to the gifts. And no thanks to you. Nice meeting you. Then carry on to work and on with *my life. I really blew that job. I had to go to work bruised and battered.*

- *All his Exes were crazy. Everybody wants him and hits on him (including men). His family is all dumb and he is always right. Early Love Bombing. Wanted everything fast (but asked me if he was going too fast that he would "tone it down"). That I was always guarded.*

- *My intuition felt that something was wrong from the beginning in his behavior, but I did not want to judge too harshly or be seen as being kind of prissy. I thought he was simply insecure in showing love because of his own difficult childhood. After all this, it feels like I broke my own neck with my never-ending empathy and sympathy.*

- *Wanting to see me every evening in the first two weeks of dating, telling me for the first time he loved me over the phone and being generous with gifts. And the list goes on and on.*

- *I still see and feel ALL the red flags but why do I feel my higher self is guiding me to hang in there? Every time I start the process to leave ALWAYS a situation arises that guides me back???*

- *I should have listened to my first instincts about the evil Narc troll, seeing him as the loser that he truly was. I would have realized that I couldn't "save" him or "help" him to be a good person. I would have paid attention to those nagging feelings I had about him in the beginning, the ones that I excused and ignored because the love bombing was so nice.*

- *He talked about marriage after a month of being together*

- *He wanted to marry me twice in the 4 years and even that felt wrong. It meant absolutely nothing for him, simply future faking...*

- *Mine was far too interested in my past partners*

- *They seem to find ones who they know they can slowly and subtly abuse, as they get their kicks from it. It was 23 years of ignoring the red flags until one really hit me over the head. An incredible story but as I am sure that many can relate, mine stemmed from untreated trauma in childhood. My poor mother did the best she could and I emulated her life and it was for a short time, just after she was diagnosed with cancer that we really had a connection of knowing that neither one of us had been living authentically.*

- *He wanted to be with me 24/7 and when I had my second baby, I wasn't allowed to be on my own with him! He also told me he was too proud to claim benefits but yet didn't find a job, so he used my child's money.*

These came from people who have lived the horror and are just a fraction of the examples I've heard, but I wanted to share them as a way of authenticating everything that you'll read about in this book.

Let's get back to more Red Flags, though I'm not quite done with love bombing yet.

Red Flag No 5: Emotional Seduction – love bombing by a different name

Not all romantic predatory narcissists are overly sexual. The somatic is, but there are many variations of narcissistic personalities as I've explained, and some of them, such as cerebral and vulnerable narcissists, don't care for sex at all. At a push they can and will perform, but it's not what drives their engine. This is where emotional seduction comes in, and even in the case of the somatic, if the target is backing off and not giving in to their initial sexual advances, they'll employ this tactic in spades too.

Narcissists are adept at listening, reading people, mirroring and very quickly creating a powerful bond between the two of you. When you're talking, they seem captivated by everything you say, they ask lots of questions (often too many – see Red Flag No 8, below), and you keep thinking 'Wow! We've got so much in common! They're LIKE me and THEY LIKE me! They GET me!' The more you talk, the more synchronicity there seems to be. It's amazing! Unbelievable! Fantastic! Except it's not. It's all fake.

Here's an example in action! As I was in the process of writing this book, I had a post in my Facebook Support Group, which clearly demonstrates how this can show up – I'd identify this as a vulnerable narcissist (VN) and I've shown the Red Flags in brackets:

"I just separated from my cheating hubby who has narcissistic characteristics. After 5 months of separation I met a very nice guy that actually made me feel really good about myself. (1) I was honest with him from the start (2) and he also came out of a long-term relationship. We hit it off right from the start because we had so much in common.(3) I learned he's been exactly where I'm at! He spoke about what he went through and it was like I was looking in a mirror reflection of what I was going through...(4)

To make a long story short... as the weeks passed he became clingy and always reminded me why I shouldn't allow my husband back in my life. (VN) Everything he said made perfect sense... until I noticed his rage outbursts when I asked about certain things...(5) It didn't alert me yet but then it started happening often. (6) Then the give away... he started to dictate to me what I should do but then say "I'm not trying to dictate what you should do"... (7) and (VN)

How to avoid the trap – My Advice

Call 'Time out' in your head. Say 'STOP!' And ask yourself: 'Is this for real? What are the chances?' Because IT IS both amazing and unbelievable, when you know what's really going on behind the scenes – or rather, underneath the fake persona, the façade, of the narcissist and all this fantastic synchronicity.

When that mask slips, what you'll witness is very ugly indeed and you're going to pay the price for causing it to slip because you are NOT perfect. You're just a normal human being, God love you and when ugly reality shows up, it's going to turn your world horribly upside down. So don't let it happen, know the signs, I can't say it enough – trust your gut! I'm glad to say that the woman whose example I've shared realized within a month that she was dealing with a narcissist and she *'bumped his sorry ass instantly'!'* I was delighted to hear it!

Red Flag No 6: They seem to 'instinctively' know a LOT about you!

Most narcissists select their targets based on a set of personal characteristics that they know, if a person has these, they will fall for their fake charm. They seek a certain kind of person, one who is empathetic, forgiving, kind, spiritual, loving, generous, or vulnerable in some way – perhaps someone who has low self-esteem or lacks confidence. The latter make particularly good targets because they will be such easy prey for the narcissist; it is like lambs to the slaughter.

But how do they do this? Simple. They research you before targeting you. They want to know they have a fighting chance of ensnaring you. Ironically, narcissists are very economical with how much energy they wish to expend and they only want to expend it if they know they have a very high chance of getting their much-needed life-blood, narcissistic supply (or fuel), from you. They will have spotted you somewhere - it could be in the 'real' world, or online, and then they will start researching you. So, let's have a look at how they do it.

Your Friends

Unbeknownst to you, a narcissist or one of their Lieutenants may get to know one or two of your friends, just to pump them for information about you. They may even orchestrate it so that one of them introduces you to the narcissist. One of the reasons why they are very keen to meet your friends as soon as possible (see Red Flag No 17) is because your friends are rich sources of information about you. They won't know that everything they innocently share about you is being filed away in the narcissist's mind. They are experts at engaging your friends in conversation under the guise of being so happy they have met you and just want to know everything about you. Your friends will not suspect a thing.

Social Media

The first and easiest way to find out a LOT about a total stranger is of course, social media (SM). 'Friend' request or 'Follow' have a lot to answer for. If you have an online presence, it's a piece of cake for anyone to find out tons of information about your likes and dislikes, things you care about, places you like to go and your friends will be unwittingly/unknowingly drawn into providing more info about you.

Silent Stalking

They will show up and watch you from afar, in a bar, restaurant, or anywhere that you frequent. Of course, you won't know who they are at this point, so you'll be blissfully unaware that a romantic predator is silently stalking you. You're in no danger at this stage, but if you match the criteria they are looking for, then big trouble is on its way to you.

The Narcissist's Army: Lieutenants

Now here's one you won't have heard of, and neither had I. This much lesser-known tactic of employing 'Lieutenants' is described in great detail by HG Tudor in his book, 'Sitting Target: How and Why the Narcissist Chooses You' and in his blog post, 'The Narcissist's Army'. They are NOT to be confused with flying monkeys because those are a different breed, which I cover in Red Flag No 46.

Basically, this is where they send out envoys or scouts – the narcissist's admirers/supporters - to ascertain your suitability as a potential source of 'fuel' BEFORE they ever approach you themselves. When they move in for the kill, they are already confident that you are the right kind of person to supply them with all the fuel they will need. The scary thing is that you will probably NEVER know that you had an encounter with a narcissistic lieutenant. In fact, you won't even come across this term in the mainstream material out there, no matter how hard you try to find it. But if you think back, to before you met the narcissist or HOW you met him, you may well recall something significant, as one of my group members did:

'Whoa, wait...he asked about me in the dance crowd, a DJ friend of his had a video of me in a dance class, he gave him the video, I was flattered at the time, as no one had ever gone out of their way to know about me, now it's called 'studying you.'

And another asked me:

'Rings a bell, but how do you differentiate between a Narc and a 'normal' guy who's 'interested' in you... Because some guys don't come straight to you initially, they use other people to get your number, attention etc.... Or maybe they are Narcs as well?'

Yes indeed, maybe they are Lieutenants! The DJ was almost certainly a Lieutenant. The fact is, you can't know who is a Narc and who is 'normal', which is why you have to keep your Narc Radar on full alert if you are on the dating scene or looking for love. The only place this staple tactic of the narcissist has been revealed is in Tudor's work. I highly recommend you read the book because it will make your eyes water and they won't be tears of joy. I'll post links in the 'Reading and Resources' Section at the end of the book.

It's not difficult for them to find out where you live (or at least, roughly where), what school you went to, your job history, where you work, what music you like, restaurants you frequent, foods you like and so on, by using their Lieutenants. And of course, we all share so much on SM these days, but in doing so we never know that our genuine interests and day-to-day lives could be under surveillance by a romantic predatory narcissist and his or her lieutenants. It's such an ugly thought, but the reality is far uglier.

Remember that they are PREDATORS… they will scout you, stalk you, corner you and move in for the kill. And you are the fragile, helpless creature who's going to get caught in their hideous trap.

How to avoid the trap - my advice

Be suspicious if someone seems to know a lot about you or your likes, dislikes, on first meeting you. Instead of just thinking 'potential narcissist ', you need to be thinking 'lieutenant primed?' Because you've very probably been pre-screened by one of them. Listen carefully to the little alarm bells ringing, that have you wondering 'Hmm… how did he/she know that?' How indeed! Think immediately of what I'm sharing in this book. They may well be genuine, but until you KNOW this for sure, keep your detective radar up and don't fall for it.

To lie or not to lie, that is the question

If you start to feel that this person seems fake, try a few 'tricks'. Now, I'm not suggesting that lying is a good thing and I know that it goes against your integrity, which is not something I'd encourage you to do, but I do believe that there's a time and a place and 'white lies' have their uses. I would only suggest doing this if you are getting some strong vibes that this person could be a narcissist and you want to test the waters a bit more. So here's a way to do this, **IF** you feel confident and comfortable doing so – I understand not everyone will, but I remember way back in my dating days (long before I'd ever heard the word narcissist) when guys would be chatting me up and I'd just get this feeling that they were bullshitters, so this is what I used to do!

Casually mention something that you 'love to do', but in fact have never done, or have no desire whatsoever to do. For example, 'Oh, I haven't done it in ages, but I absolutely love kayaking/white water rafting/rock climbing (or something completely different if you happen to love these things – I'm just using them as an example). And see if 'Person Perfect' gushes that they also love this too.

Then, push the boundaries. But do it casually. Think of something else you can also pretend to 'love', but actually can't stand... a place, a celebrity, food, drink, anything along those lines, and talk about how much you love/enjoy and look forward to going/watching/eating etc. again... and watch as the synchronicity emerges again... and again, and again. Basically, take a leaf out of their book and be 'fake' for a while, knowing exactly what you are doing. If the person in front of you is a narcissist, it will become very obvious to you, very quickly. There is nothing better than playing someone at their own game... and winning. Whenever I did this with guys who'd chat me up, I would always know they were liars because they agreed with everything I said, and even back in my 20s I knew that just wasn't normal.

If YOUR Narc Radar is on full alert, you'll see that there is nothing you can come up with that the Narc doesn't agree to like or dislike as much as you do. But don't be too obvious about this. You can also do this with things you really love, but pretend you don't. Let's say you love a good massage… most people do and that's expected. But you say you don't. Say you find it uncomfortable to have strangers touching you. **Play them at their own game**. Be subtle, especially if you're still not sure after say, the first or second date, and want to scope them out some more. Keep adding up the Red Flags. Keep your guard up and don't share anything too personal.

Remember I mentioned 'white lies'? Lie through your back and front teeth! When you are trying to figure out if a person is a narcissist, you have to be as cunning as they are. Listen to everything that comes out of their mouth. How realistic is all this? Then mentally sit back, relax and look at the bigger picture of what's going on, and don't allow yourself to be bedazzled by how attractive this person is or how attracted you are to them. Or how sweet and vulnerable they seem. Always be asking yourself, 'Who is this person, really?' and assert your right to take time to get to know them at your own pace and on your own terms.

And what about the Lieutenants?

These people are just as deadly – more deadly in their own way because they will usually be average looking, nice and pleasant enough, and you'll have no reason to be suspicious of them, so your guard will be down and you'll share all kinds of information that will be filtered back to the narcissist.

In the case of the Lieutenants, there isn't a lot you can do unless you want to lock yourself away in a convent, refuse to engage with any new people ever again or just lie about everything to every new person you meet (none of which are ideal or sustainable solutions). Could all this make you a tad (or a LOT) paranoid? Initially, I think yes, it absolutely could, especially if you've been in a narcissistic relationship and know what can happen because you've suffered the abuse. You don't trust yourself, your intuition, and you are running fearful about so much and you are understandably terrified of trusting anyone. It will take time to learn to be able to trust and love again. This is why I also recommend that you do NOT get back into the dating scene until you are fully healed, restored and armed with a whole new set of skills and information that will enable you to protect yourself from future harm.

But when you are ready, tune into yourself from the very beginning when you start dating a new man or woman. Your feelings are your barometer that help you to sense danger. And in the case of a Romantic Predator, that barometer is trying to tell you something. It's your job to love and respect yourself enough to listen to it. Trust yourself. You KNOW what you're doing and you're hearing these alarm bells for a reason.

In fact, your emotional barometer is always there to guide you, throughout the relationship, so it's always wise to tune in and ask how are you feeling? Are you being heard, are your needs being met or are you feeling uneasy all the time? Make it a point to do this regularly and scratch beneath the surface. Narcissists have a way of gradually eroding your sense of self, your reality and of getting you to manage down your expectations so that you're settling for less and less as time goes on. If you keep tuning in, you'll realize that unhappiness is bubbling away inside you, waiting for you to pay attention and do something about it.

Red Flag No 7: They brag, boast and name-drop

Overt and covert narcissists think they are superior to everyone else, regardless of reality, so they will boast of how successful, important and valuable they are at work, in business, and frankly, in everything. They hold this mental image of themselves as all this being true and will waste no time in telling boastful stories about all kinds of things that have gone on at work or elsewhere, how priceless they are and that the company would be in big trouble without them. They also 'seem' to be experts in so many areas. Any subject that comes up (often they will bring it up), they'll dazzle you with accolades of their knowledge and brilliance. All of this can be nicely summed up in one word: arrogance. It's a personality trait I have disliked in people since I was old enough to understand that people could be different.

They name drop. This is due to their need for admiration and being seen as important and above your average 'Joe or Jane'. They want to impress you because that means you're going to give them positive fuel with your reaction, and because you're so caught up in them, you don't see it as bragging. You're gushing all over them. (Or maybe you're not actually gushing, but still, you're thinking Wow!) 'They've got Ed Sheeran on speed dial!' It's all bullshit. One woman I talked to told me her ex, who was a musician, showed her Ed's name and number in his phone. She eventually found out it was a bogus number and he'd never met him.

How to avoid the trap – My advice

In the back of your mind, perhaps you're already thinking 'Wow, this person is really arrogant', but you stop listening to your gut because you want a relationship so badly, you're prepared to overlook way too much. Maybe you just want to believe this gorgeous person simply because they are gorgeous. But take a mental step back again, and ask yourself why is this person sharing all this information that only points to them being so brilliant? Ask yourself my favorite question: Who DOES that? This is a very simple question but it's very effective because when you ask yourself a question, your brain goes into 'scan mode' to find the answer. It's looking for a match to pair up with your question. So, remember this question and use it. What will happen is one of two things:

1. Your internal scanner will find a match to some other arrogant or obnoxious person and you will remember that you didn't like or trust that person either

2. Your internal scanner will not be able to find a match. You don't know ANYBODY who does this. This automatically makes this person suspect.

So, ask that question, and remember Red Flag No 1: Trust your gut! If they seem boastful and braggy at this stage, this is who they are. This person is a narcissist. It will get worse and you'll rue the day you ever met Polly or Peter Perfect if you don't listen to your intuition.

Red Flag No 8: They want to know EVERYTHING about you

When you meet a new person, it's normal to talk about simple things, like the weather, what might be going on where you're meeting, 'how often do you come here' and other light fare. On a first date, you generally keep the conversation light. Where are you from? What do you do for a living? How long have you lived here? And so on. First dates (or even second or third dates) are not about finding out a person's entire life history in one sitting. But it can seem like that with a narcissist.

Under the guise of being fascinated with you, they will bombard you with questions and will want to know everything about your life for as far back as you can remember. They'll want to know about your past loves, sex life, childhood, relationships with your family, etc. And they want to know the deep, nitty-gritty of all of it! Because you're so enchanted with them at this point, you'll want to build more trust, and the easiest and most natural way to do that is to share your secrets. You interpret this as them being so interested and caring, wanting to know you much better, so you'll spill all your secrets, hurts, fears and hopes. Remember that you are in the hands of a skilled manipulator who knows exactly what they are doing and how to extract this information from you.

How to avoid the trap - my advice

Don't share personal information with them. Keep in mind that they are very probably 'mining for gold' to use against you at a future date. Be very, very careful what you share with them at this stage. RESIST – with all of your might, the urge to share anything that is deeply emotional or painful for you. Remind yourself that though you're head-over-heels in love, it is still very early days and you simply don't know enough about them to share your innermost secrets.

One woman in my group asked me 'What counts as personal information? Do I tell him that I have 3 siblings and I'm divorced?' My answer was yes, you can tell him that, but if you have troubled relationships with any family members, do NOT share that. If he asks why you got divorced, do NOT go into details. Say something like 'Oh you know, like a lot of marriages, it just didn't work out.' If he pushes for more info, just say you'd rather talk about something else. Keep it light – like, 'Hey, can we talk about something else?'

BUT: Be careful with your choice of words. If you're tempted to say something that you've probably often been advised to say from other sources, such as 'I don't feel comfortable talking about it' – DON'T say that! Why? Because saying you're 'not comfortable' with something is a dead giveaway to a narcissist.. Because maybe deep down, you're really unhappy about the break-up, and if you are, the Narc's radar will be on full alert and you'll have given them a clue that they won't forget. They will file this away in their devious little mind and they will come back to it when they've gained a bit more of your trust. It's a potential vulnerable button that they will one day push just to cause you pain.

Don't give them that. Keep your cards close to your chest. If they keep pushing, you could also say 'That's a boundary issue for me.' (I'll talk about boundaries in a short while because that's another biggie.) Be firm. Move the conversation onto something more neutral. If you're the kind of person who's not great at spontaneous conversation, write out a list of things that you can talk about easily. Art? Books? Movies? TED Talks? Pick easy subjects you know a fair bit about and can talk about comfortably.

When you say, 'I'd rather not talk about it', watch for their reaction to this. They will either brush it off and feign innocence with something like 'Oh but I SO want to know and understand you better', and they may add a coy 'I hope you'll soon learn to trust me enough to share your feelings with me.' Or, they'll take a more defensive stance and feign hurt that you don't trust them. Boo-hoo!

What's going on here in both cases is they're trying to get you to believe in them and trust them, so they can gain more information about you to use against you at a future date. In the first case, they're sugar-coating it and by adding that they hope you'll soon learn to trust them, they're playing a subtle guilt-game to guilt-trip you into feeling bad that you don't trust them. This will have you second-guessing yourself and feeling that you're not giving enough to this amazing new potential relationship.

In the second case, their objective is EXACTLY the same and you'll feel the same way... guilty that you're not trusting and giving in this potential relationship.

And there's a third possibility. They may say, 'Ok, I understand... but is it ok if I share some of mine with you?' Watch out for this one because what comes out of their mouths next is very likely to be lies or at the very least, gross fabrications of the truth. A parent, or whoever may well have abused them, but the reality will not be the story you're about to hear. This kind of early self-disclosure will be embellished to get the sympathy vote from you. And their objective will be to gain your trust (therefore, you'll share your 'stuff') because they've shared their innermost secrets with you. The law of reciprocal altruism kind of kicks in here! It's a cunning ploy, but very simple to spot when you know what to look for.

When you don't know what you are looking for, they will have skillfully emotionally manipulated you into feeling bad about yourself for not trusting them, so you then soften up inside and tell them everything. Bingo! Score big time for the narcissist. And now you've exposed a vulnerability that they are going to use against you in the future. And they will. If you've lost a child, a beloved pet, had an abortion that you still feel guilty about, were sexually abused, they will throw it into your face and say that you deserved it. Nothing is sacred in the hands of a narcissist. Absolutely nothing. Remember that these people are truly unconscionable and the things they do make a normal person shudder at just the thought.

Here is an example that shows how this might work, shared with me from a member of my group. This was on a dating site where the person who shared it had only recently connected with this man:

'I lived with my grandparents for the first 7 years of my life. My grandmother was everything to me. I still have her family heirloom pin that I wear on my coat. We were inseparable. She said she did not want me being raised in a dysfunctional family environment.

My parents were a mess. My mother tried to be a good mother. She was very loving and affectionate, but she couldn't handle her own life, let along the life of her children. My father was wildly abusive and hateful. He should never have married or had children. His life was not well lived. If there was ever a pathetic person, it was him and his life.

My father died in 1992 and my mother in 2011. I had a wonderful sister who was 9 years older than me. She was killed in a gruesome car accident in 1970. Grandma and I relied on each other for strength and support. Grandma died in 1974. So in 4 years, I lost the two most loving, supportive people in my life. I have always relied on my strong faith to help me endure bad times...

I don't have a medical background, I'm just familiar with a lot of mental health disorders, probably because of the dysfunctional relationships in my life. I don't know how to handle everything but I am fairly well-equipped to deal with mental health problems...

Feel free to ask me any questions that you may have about me and my past. If you are curious, it will be good for you to ask many questions so that you can satisfy your curiosity...'

Do you see the clever emotional manipulation going on here? If not, let me deconstruct it for you! First paragraph immediately fires off an image in your head of a cute little 7-year-old boy with his loving Grandma. He still wears her pin in loving memory. How sweet! They were 'inseparable'. This has set him up as this kind, Grandma-loving guy! But, how weird is it for a grown man to say he was 'inseparable' from his Grandmother? Then he leads into his dysfunctional family by saying how his Grandma didn't want him to be raised in such a family.

Paragraph 2, he gets right into the typical dysfunctional, abusive father and the downtrodden mother incapable of looking after herself, or her children. Paragraph 3, we learn he had a 'loving' sister, who was killed in a 'gruesome' car accident. This paragraph reveals a lot: Flag 1: ALL of these people are now DEAD. Flag 2: Who says 'gruesome' car accident? It's a word designed to bring an image of his 'loving' sister, broken and bloody, in this 'gruesome' accident. This is designed to evoke your sympathy for this guy who has lost all these people, but in case you're in any doubt, he makes it clear at the end.

3rd paragraph. He doesn't have a medical background, but he's 'well-equipped' to deal with mental health problems'. Huge Red Flag here. This is making you think that he's really going to understand YOUR emotional problems and you're going to have such synchronicity with him because of HIS suffering.

Last paragraph, he invites you to ask him anything you want. This is a ploy to make you think he's open, honest and willing to share ANYTHING with you. This will immediately tap into your subconscious need to give back what you think he's given to you, so you will start sharing all your personal 'stuff' with him.

But the biggest Red Flag outside of what's revealed in his message WHEN you know what to look for, is the simple one of why? Why would someone you've only just connected with start sharing all this deeply personal information with you? It is more than likely all lies anyway. Do NOT fall for these ploys!

In the first and second examples I mentioned earlier, when they are using these ploys to try to get you to open up, say, 'Yes, maybe in time' and brush it off. But in your mind be thinking, 'This woman/man has not earned the right to know these personal things about my life. I don't care how gorgeous/sexy/whatever he/she is, that's over-stepping the mark'. You could also confront them and ask them why they are asking such personal questions when they don't know you, or have only just met you?

We are taught by and large, to be pleasant when we meet people, so often, even when we feel something is wrong, or off, we'll sidestep it just to stay 'pleasant' but frankly, if someone is pushing for personal information at this stage, there's nothing wrong with telling them to back off. This is about protecting your boundaries (more of which coming up in Red Flag No 12) as much as it is about social etiquette. Keep your cards close to your chest again, until this person has proven, beyond a shadow of a doubt, that they have earned your trust. Listen and nod sympathetically, but don't fall for the ploy and start sharing your hurtful, painful past.

On this note, if they have shared their sob story with you, ask yourself why would someone you have just met or barely know, do this? Red Flags waving in the wind again. Even if there is SOME truth in it, why do they feel the need to share it with you so early on in the relationship? People just don't do this.

After closing the door on the conversation about things you don't want to talk about, ask yourself is it 'normal' for a person to be so intensely curious about your life? Normal people don't go into deep, intimate, emotional 'stuff' so early on in a relationship. It takes time to build up trust and time to feel comfortable asking people deeply personal, intimate questions about their lives (and that includes sexual history and preferences). Ask yourself if this is really appropriate?

Give yourself the gift of more time to get to know them better. Keep observing their behavior and keep your guard up. I know this can be really hard, especially when they seem so wonderful and caring, you're having an amazing time with them and you just want them to really know you. But you have to keep thinking ahead. There is still a LOT you need to know about them before you can trust them. And the sad fact is, a narcissist can keep up this lovely façade for a long time. So that's why you need to be aware, and on the lookout, for the other Red Flags ALL the time.

One more thing: Remember I said that they have researched you and they may know a lot more about you than you realize. If they have, the advantage YOU have here is that they can't let on that they know it, other than using manipulative ploys to convince you that they just 'knew' or 'just felt it' from you. If this happens, see that big Red Flag blowing in the wind and keep your Narc radar on high alert.

Red Flag No 9: They want to know NOTHING about you

On the flip side, if you're meeting an overt narcissist for a first date, they may not want to know anything about you and will spend the whole evening talking about themselves, discussing the wine as if they are sommeliers, the menu as if they were chefs, being condescending to the waiters, and insisting on choosing dinner and wine for both of you. Because they know best, you see and they'll tell you that. They want to make all the choices, and it doesn't matter that YOU might not like what they order for you.

You could get through a whole evening without them asking you a single question about yourself. If you have any sense, you'll see them for what they are: Obnoxious, self-absorbed bores and you'll never want to see them again. But remember, narcissists have a way of getting their hooks into you and if you let them, they will. Even if you think they are arrogant and awful on this first date, you're still not safe. Perhaps you just really fancy them, or in a weak moment when you find the weekend looming with nothing to do and a text arrives from them, you might just think 'What the heck. I'll give them another chance.' And that second chance could be all they need to turn their charm on you. That will be your fatal mistake.

How to avoid the trap – my advice.

Do NOT mistake this arrogance for confidence or think that they are being 'chivalrous'. They are being domineering and controlling. And if they are like this on a first date, just allow yourself to imagine what they'll be like once they get you under their full control. Because that is their ultimate aim. They want to control you so that they can use and abuse you. An overt narcissist is like a juggernaut running over a tricycle - it's going to be crushed flat. As you will be if you get into a relationship with one.

If they are like this on a first date, message them 'Thanks for a nice evening but I don't feel we're suited.' And block their number as soon as you've sent it. Block them from your dating site and SM. Do NOT give them that second chance to come back at you. Don't look back.

Red Flag No 10: They are alone – but why?

If this person is so gorgeous, clever, funny, generous, (those ones who insist on picking up the tab or paying for your drinks at the bar in the early stages), why are they alone? You must ask yourself this. Now of course, there are tons of gorgeous people out there who are single and searching, but this book is about helping you to spot a narcissist and avoid the trap, so this is a question you need to be asking yourself. Why has this gorgeous individual not been snapped up? Why are they in a bar (or wherever), alone?

How to avoid the trap – my advice

Obviously, you will have checked and noticed no wedding ring, but don't take this at face value. Narcissists frequently remove their wedding rings and if there's no telltale suntan ring mark, you have no way of knowing whether they are married or not. Even if they are not married, you can be sure that they are dating at least one other person, and in the process of discarding another. Narcissists typically have several relationships on the go at any one time because they are serial cheaters and they are extremely good at hiding this. You can ask, of course, but you have no way of knowing if they are lying. You're going to have to do some subtle detective work of your own.

This brings me to the next Red Flag, as it can pop up here, and it usually pops up repeatedly in the relationship later too.

Red Flag No 11: They trash their Exes

It's fairly common and acceptable when you're on a first date to ask a person if they've been married or how long they've been on the dating scene. If they've asked you (and you've told them you're divorced, recently broken up or whatever, there's your opportunity to bounce it back and ask 'and how about you?'), listen carefully to how they talk about their Exes as you probe to find the answer to why they are alone. Was it all the ex's fault? Does this person talk their Ex down? Describe him/her as 'crazy/jealous/unhinged' or any other kind of negative description? As you dig deeper, you'll see a pattern of a LOT of Exes, and a lot of trash talk about them.

They may play the hurt, rejected, 'broken-hearted over the break-up' card. Do they make themselves out to be the victim of a scheming, unkind, cruel ex? They are still trashing their ex, but in a way that makes you feel sorry for them.

Do they go the complete opposite way and wax lyrical about how amazing this person was? How sorry they are that it didn't work out? Usually, it's more likely to be the former, but it could be the latter – and the latter is something that often shows up later in your relationship with them, and I'll go into that in a bit more detail in Red Flag No 29.

How to avoid the trap – my advice

How they talk about their Ex is a critical clue to what's really going on with them. Most people – normal people – don't go into details about their Ex at this point. If you're getting too much information, beware. Something much more sinister could be going on behind this story you're being told. Everything they are saying has a hidden agenda to make YOU feel a certain way. Their story is aimed at either getting you to feel sorry for them and setting up a construct in your mind that you'd never do that to them, or it's designed to push your nurturing, empathetic buttons to want to heal all that hurt. It's a clever manipulative tactic and because the narcissist is a master at this game, you'll have no clue unless you KNOW the ploys and have YOUR Narc Radar on full alert.

If they start saying nasty things about their ex, no matter how kind their approach, don't believe them. There are two sides to every story and you're only hearing what they want you to hear. And again, ask yourself why they would talk badly about their Ex when they've only just met you? Imagine them talking about YOU like this 6 months down the line. A genuine, decent person doesn't start trashing their Ex to the first person they meet. Most relationships break up because the people in them couldn't work things out and many relationships break up amicably, but even if they didn't, normal people do NOT want to start dishing the dirt and going over the awfulness of the previous relationship with a potential new partner. It's just not the way it should go, so if it's going that way, put your Narc Radar on high alert, and put your emotional brakes on.

If they are idealizing their ex, telling you how wonderful they were in every way, and how sad they are that it didn't work out, why would anyone say that on a date? Who does this? But they DO say it! This should be telling you loud and clear that something is wrong. If you get into a relationship with this person, you're setting yourself up for constant abuse in the form of comparison, among many other dreadful things that I cover as you delve deeper into this book.

You will be compared and found wanting in every department. You won't be as attractive as the iconic ex, you won't be as fit, your body won't be as good, you won't be as intelligent, you won't be as good in bed, you won't be as good at your job... you won't be as good at yada, yada, yada and this type of abuse will slowly erode your sense of self-worth. You will keep trying to live up to these unattainable (and totally false) ideals of perfection that are being constantly shoved in your face. Before long, you'll feel fat, ugly and unlovable – even if you are slim, gorgeous and have a heart of gold. Believe me, I have women in my group sending me pictures of themselves and they are stunning; yet their sense of self-worth has been so systematically destroyed, that they really believe they are unattractive. Their reality - and yours, if you don't heed all the warnings in this book - will be completely changed to a false new reality of the narcissist's making.

Pay very close attention to how they talk about their Ex because it will give you a lot of valuable information about what kind of person they are. Is this the kind of person you want to get involved with? Would you talk about any of your Exes in the same way? If they way they are talking sounds wrong to you, file it under FLAG and block them. You definitely don't want another date with this person.

Red Flag No 12: They have no respect for your boundaries

This actually fits into the love bombing stage too. It's such a big issue, not just in the potential Romantic Predator stages, but in many other areas of your life. In this situation, checking boundaries is one of the easiest 'tests' you can apply to determine if a narcissist is in fact a narcissist. This is because they all have this inherent sense of entitlement to have, be and do whatever they want, whenever they want. They don't recognize boundaries and will gatecrash any you might put in place. They will bombard you with texts, emails, turn up at all hours at your home or place of work and this behavior is rife as I've explained, during the 'Love Bombing' phase in Red Flag No 4.

What makes you throw your 'boundaries' caution to the wind is, of course, how in love or infatuated you are with them. It feels SO good to have this delightful new individual suddenly obsessed with you. You're soaking up all this love and adoration because it feels so damn good to be desired in this way. You're feeling on top of the world and who can blame you? We all want to be loved and adored! These feelings make it all that much easier for the narcissist to smash those boundaries to smithereens.

How to avoid the trap – My advice

Set your personal boundaries and Deal Breakers

Set your personal boundaries right from the start of the relationship. If you don't want to hear from them – by text or any other way – say, after 10pm at night, make that clear, and if they ignore it and call or text you, ignore it, or better yet, turn your phone off if you have no valid reason to keep it on, or put it on silent. And file that boundary buster under FLAG!

Train yourself from the start to NOT dance to this person's tune. Consider instead that every time they call or text, they are in effect demanding your attention. Your attention, adoration and admiration are what a narcissist needs. Think instead about YOUR needs. Yes, this person is gorgeous, but if they are not RESPECTING your requests this early on, ask yourself why? If someone truly loves you, their first concern should be your comfort and they absolutely should be willing to respect your wishes. Don't fall for the love bombing bullshit; it's just not real. If you've had that from them and now your boundaries are being crashed, you're heading fast into 'Narcland' - unless you put a stop to it – FAST.

Set times and places to meet

Dates should only happen when you've both agreed on a time and place to meet. If they turn up unexpectedly at your home, make it very clear that you've not agreed to this and you don't want them showing up unexpectedly. Watch how they react to this. Do they accept it, apologize and go away or do they start saying that they missed you, thought you'd be happy to see them, are upset that you're rejecting them knowing how they feel about you? All of this should have alarm bells screaming in your head. Do NOT fall for this. Tell them politely that you have a life and you have plans or things to do. Now I'd advise you if you've had the love bombing and then this, to end it. Right now.

If they turn up at your place of work as you're leaving, or at a bar or restaurant where you're out with friends... be suspicious. Red Flag No 13 will clarify why.

List your Deal Breakers

Think about your boundaries and what is most important to you in the early stages and indeed, in the later stages, of a relationship. Make a list of your top 5 Deal Breakers and while you're at it, make a list of the 'Core Values' that are important to you in a relationship. These should be things that matter deeply to you, such as loyalty, honesty, integrity, respect, kindness and so on. Put them side-by-side in columns and keep checking them against the behavior of your new beau. Do they measure up or are they starting to show their true colors? Remember that abuse can only happen if you allow it. It's your job to protect yourself. Do NOT share or discuss this with them. This is you doing your private analysis and anything you share with them is liable to be used to draw you deeper in. Don't give them any extra help!

Red Flag No 13: They have an explanation for everything!

Narcissists are quick thinkers, but more often than not, they will already have planned and thought through their 'spontaneous' arrivals and answers to any questions you might have so they'll always be ready with an answer for you.

Let's say they happen to be walking up the street as you are leaving work. Wow, what a coincidence! 'How nice to see you!' they'll say and beam a smile at you. 'I was just on my way to X! What are you doing here?' You tell them you work here, and they feign surprise. But they are lying – they've already researched you and they know exactly where you work and hang out.

They turn up at a bar you frequent, again feigning surprise and delight to see you there. 'Wow, I've been here so many times. I can't believe I didn't notice you before.' they say with total conviction. But they have noticed you and all along they were planning their strategy. Or, possibly it's the first time they've been there and they are only there because they know you are.

They'll tell you that they have noticed you in this place many times, and loved you from afar from the first time they saw you; that they've been trying to work up the courage to talk to you for ages. That's another Red Flag waving in the wind. If you hear this from them, ask yourself why would it take them so long to work up the courage to approach you? Especially if they are the good-looking, confident type. The Vulnerable narcissist might get away with this, so be on the lookout for this Red Flag if you're dealing with a vulnerable, shy type.

As time goes on, you'll realize that they always have an explanation for everything. Narcissists have a way with words. It's often called 'word salad' and cerebrals, especially, can run verbal rings round anyone, applying bizarre techniques of circular logic and argumentative reasoning that would baffle the greatest scientific minds in the world today. If you get deeply entrenched in a relationship with them, they'll swear black is white, day is night, dogs are cats and they'll twist your reality into something you don't recognize any more. What's so much worse is that they will twist YOU into someone you don't recognize any more.

How to avoid the trap – My advice

If this person turns up at your work unexpectedly, just ask yourself 'Is this really a coincidence, or did they plan it?' Keep an open mind. Don't let on you are suspicious; just keep your mind open to the possibility. Remember you are still at the 'adding up the Red Flags' stage. File this under Red Flag too.

If they turn up at bars, restaurants etc., repeatedly, and they seem to have a viable explanation every time, do the same thing. It's easy, just be open in your own mind to the possibility that you could be a target who is potentially being groomed by a narcissistic romantic predator. Be suspicious; if you're wrong you won't have lost anything, but if this type of behavior is going on you're not wrong. How many Red Flags have you filed by now? If you've got more than 3, it's time to call a halt and end this 'relationship.'

Red Flag No 14: YOU are a Red Flag... if you're an Empath or Highly Sensitive Person (HSP) - 10 common traits

If you are an Empath or HSP, your risk of attracting a narcissist is WAY higher than if you are not! In fact, you're the Holy Grail, the pot of gold at the end of the rainbow, for a narcissist. They KNOW what you are, and they know they can manipulate all your good qualities and use them against you as soon as they reach the devaluing stage. You're exactly what they are looking for.

As an Empath myself, (I score 15 out of 20 Traits on Judith Orloff's assessment) this deeply offends me. How dare they take advantage and exploit the good, kind and loving qualities you have and use them to manipulate and destroy you? I was utterly furious when I first learned this. I've never been subjected to narcissistic abuse myself. The closest I got was 7 years with a man who had Borderline Personality Disorder and though he was never abusive, some freaky s*** happened and I ended the relationship, after which he met a new woman and got her pregnant within a week, and completely cut me out of his life as if I'd never existed. I also believe in past lives and I'm sure I've been both a narcissist and a victim in my past lives; that deep knowledge fires my passion for the subject and my need to help people in this life!

In this life I have learned how to protect myself from negative energy and emotional vampires and I teach my clients how to do the same. I'm an Empath with very thick skin and excellent intuition. I'm also extremely good at detecting bullshit and you can be too. One of the main reasons I wrote this book was to arm all you lovely Empaths, HSPs and just nice people, with the information you need to protect yourselves from emotional vampires and narcissistic predators.

In case you've never considered this, I'm putting it in bold: **The fact is, being an empath/HSP makes YOU a Red Flag.** I will cover some of the most common 'empath/HSP' traits here, and briefly explain why these traits make you ultra-vulnerable to a narcissist. Empaths can be anywhere on the 'Empathy Spectrum', so you may only have some of these traits.

1. Empaths are highly sensitive

They're sensitive to environment, emotions, colors, sounds, lighting, smells, noise and of course, people. They can usually 'tune in' very quickly to another person's emotional wavelength. They are known for their ability to absorb other people's feelings and emotions - this is probably the most commonly cited trait of an Empath.

Why this is delightful for a narcissist and deadly for you and the truth you need to realize. I'm going to point these out for each trait!

This is delightful for a narcissist because they are excellent at reading, mimicking and mirroring people. This, coupled with the research they will have done on you prior to meeting you, is how they create powerful rapport and subsequent bonding with their 'targets'.

It's deadly for you because they actually have no genuine feelings of their own, other than their pathological need for admiration, adoration and attention, which you'll be ready and willing to give them because they are so enchanting. When you meet the narcissist, they are reflecting everything about you back to you, and *that* is what you are tuning into. A narcissist has no real self; no self exists. Effectively, you're tuning into yourself, not them. Is it any wonder that you feel this incredible connection to them?

The truth is, the person you believe to be so wonderful does NOT exist. They are a figment of their own imagination, created out of your good qualities they have temporarily borrowed from you. This is unsustainable and the mask will eventually crack, fall off, and you'll see what really lies beneath it; it's UGLY.

2. Empaths connect easily with others

Empaths are 'people persons', they love interacting and connecting with others. But often, they connect too quickly and they find it easy to 'bond' with people because they have a soul-level need to connect with people in a deep and meaningful way.

It's delightful party time for the narcissist when they meet you because you are naturally so open and willing to just be who you are and you want the connection with other people. You're super-easy to read.

It's deadly for you because you have no idea that you are facing a monster of epic proportions who is showing you a person who doesn't exist, as I've explained above. You're going to fall for a mirage of beauty who is going to turn into a beast.

And the truth is exactly what I've said, this person does not exist. They are a reflection of yourself, a projection of your good qualities. What you don't realize is, if you love yourself wholly and unconditionally for who you are at your core, you will not need validation from outside of yourself. Self-worth and self-love are key elements you need to have in place. You need to boldly love and respect yourself to the point that you don't need flattery to feel good about yourself, because you have developed a powerful innate sense of your own worth and value. I also know from my work with clients that very often, your self-worth is fragile due to a dysfunctional upbringing and if you've had one, you are even more vulnerable. See Red Flag No 15.

3. Empaths are very forgiving

Empaths are always trying to understand others, often to the point they will 'forgive', 'overlook', 'excuse' or otherwise 'accept' rude or disrespectful behavior. They'll be the ones who are always arguing against the Death Penalty, supporting Prison Reform, and generally looking for the good because they truly believe there is good in everyone.

It's delightful for narcissists because these characteristics make it very easy for them to keep abusing you, as they just know you will forgive them time and time again. They know you will accept their excuses, bad behavior and promises to change.

It's deadly for you because no matter how many times they break your heart and soul, lie, steal, cheat, even beat you, you'll forgive them and give them 'one more chance' in the hope that they will change.

The truth is, they won't change, ever. The Truth is, there is NO good in a narcissist.

4. Empaths put others before themselves

Empaths are inclined to believe that others' needs are more important than their own. This comes from their 'People Pleasing' natures.

It's delightful for narcissists because of course, this plays beautifully into their inherent belief that their needs absolutely DO come first, always, forever and a day. Narcissists are selfish in the extreme and have no capacity to understand others' feelings or needs at a genuine level. When your needs start appearing and you point out flaws in the relationship and in the narcissist, this is usually when the Devaluing starts. More on this later.

This is deadly for you because the narcissist's belief that they should always come first plays into your need to put others before you and you will go along with this because it's natural for you.

The truth is, as time goes on, you'll 'manage down' your expectations so much that you will be getting nothing, absolutely nothing, out of the relationship but abuse, abuse, and more abuse. Managing down your expectations means that you will accept less and less, being pathetically grateful for the occasional love bomb crumb. One day you'll look at yourself and wonder how the hell you got here!

5. Empaths are able to detect lies and deceptions very quickly

Uh oh! This quality takes a very long vacation when the narcissist shows up. Empaths are usually very intuitive and can pick up on negative traits in people long before others do. So why doesn't this work with a narcissist? Why does this potentially life-saving skill let them down when they need it most?

To understand this, there are two reasons I've figured out. Firstly, you have to go back and think about Empath characteristic No 1. Remember I said you're tuning into the false persona the narcissist is portraying? Effectively, tuning into yourself? At this level, there is NO deception, because the narcissist is so skilled at doing this it's un-detectable to you. They just seem to be SO on your wavelength. It's just great!

The second reason is that, of course, you're looking for love and this person enchants you. If you're hugely attracted to them and the sexual chemistry is firing up, which makes for a potent cocktail of emotions which can easily hoodwink you. There's no room for reality at this point, because this fake reality is wonderful. Except you just don't know. How could you?

It's delightful for the narcissist … I think this one is obvious, isn't it? You're easy game for the narcissist at this point.

It's deadly for you because you're being sucked into a vortex you didn't know existed and getting out of it is going to be a hell of a lot harder than it was getting in.

The truth is the only way to protect yourself from this potentially devastating harm is to take a step back and keep your emotions in check. Go over this book as many times as you need to until you know all these flags and feel them immediately when they show up. These are the emotions you need to pay attention to.

6. Empaths can be absent-minded, easily distracted and daydreamers

I've often heard Empaths described (unfairly) as 'flaky' or 'ditzy'. Because they frequently have several or all of the above characteristic traits, their emotional world can be turbulent as they try to make sense of it. Often, they lose focus and can overlook less important things and can appear to be forgetful.

This is delightful for the narcissist because it makes it so very easy to gaslight you. (See Red Flag No 30 if you're not familiar with gaslighting)

It's deadly! Holy Moly! Are you making the connection yet? As your sense of reality is constantly brought into question with gaslighting, you start doubting yourself, thinking you must be crazy, losing your mind and you're then more prone to believing everything the narcissist says at this point.

The truth is gaslighting leads to cognitive dissonance. Prolonged abuse of this kind leads to anxiety, Complex Post Traumatic Stress Disorder (C-PTSD), trauma bonding and more... all of which I'll cover in the BIG Red Flags of Narcissistic Abuse Section.

7. Empaths are deeply compassionate, selfless people

They have big hearts and look for the good in everyone. They'll try really hard to find that good, even when everyone else has walked away. They go 'all in' with relationships and don't want to give up. They'll keep hanging on, trying, hoping and believing that things will come right. They believe they have enough love to heal the narcissist.

This is delightful for the narcissist because they will milk your compassion for all its worth. They will bleed you dry of every last ounce of it.

It's deadly for you because it will emotionally exhaust you. No matter how much compassion you have to give, the narcissist will want more, and more, until you have nothing left to give. Then they will discard you, because you never meant anything to them, and as brutal as this sounds, they don't care if you live or die. I've heard the horror stories that prove it.

The truth is your compassion is wasted because nothing the narcissist says or does is real. No amount of love or compassion can ever 'fix' a narcissist. You never meant anything to them, other than your ability to provide them with narcissistic supply and they really don't care if you drop dead.

8. Empaths are 'People Pleasers' who often can't say NO

This makes them very easy to manipulate, even outside of a narcissistic relationship. They can easily be 'guilt-tripped' by family and friends into doing favors, running errands and generally being used over and above what is normal. Consequently, they are not good at setting boundaries (See Red Flag No 11).

However, I want to clarify a couple of things. The vast majority of research I've seen says that empaths are people pleasers (PP), however I couldn't find any research which showed Empaths can be NOT people pleasers. I'm an Empath, but I'm definitely not a PP! Also, it's also important to note that not all PPs are empaths. People pleasing is often a learned or adaptive behavior response often developed as a means of coping with dysfunctional parents. (See Red Flag No 15.)

This is delightful for a narcissist who believes your sole existence is to dance to their tune and attend to their every need. You were made for each other!

It's deadly for you as it leaves you no time for yourself because you're always running ragged trying to do 'stuff' for them. As an Empath, you NEED time alone to recharge your batteries. You need emotional and mental space, 'alone time' as that's a key component of being an empath. I know that I need my 'alone time' during and after family or friends' visits to my home in Spain; I'll get tired and cranky if I don't get it. I can imagine what an absolute nightmare it is to be living in a situation of constant abuse like this and getting no time to yourself.

The truth is if you're living with a narcissist, your life will never be peaceful. You'll never get healing 'alone time'. Your life will be a downward spiral that will leave you with deep emotional, psychological (and possibly physical) scars.

9. Empaths are generous

They are generous with their time, their belongings and their money.

This is delightful for narcissists because they are expert 'takers'. Their sense of entitlement is such that they genuinely believe what's yours is theirs. All of it is theirs for the taking.

This is deadly for you because they will take everything you have to give. Your home, your career, your money, your favorite personal items. They will rob you of your self-worth, self-esteem, achievements, and everything you once were. Your self-worth will be in tatters and every ounce of joy will vanish from your life.

I want to share one recent example. A woman in my Facebook Support Group told me that her Ex had persuaded her to give up her job because he didn't like her travelling every day, so she quit. At the time she contacted me, she was deep in depression, had been unable to find another job and he had discarded her. He had persuaded her to give up her life savings, $10,000, to buy him a boat, because he 'liked it so much'. Now, unable to stop checking his FB page, she saw him out on the boat with his new girlfriend, both of them all shiny, happy and smiling in the sunshine. She was absolutely devastated, still in deep denial, 'in love with him' and massively Trauma Bonded.

She told me that he had only ever been loving and kind. When I started asking her some pointed questions, the list of narcissistic abuse was so long, my head was spinning. Yet this poor woman was so brainwashed that she just could NOT see it. Cognitive dissonance and trauma bonding were out in full force. She would have taken him back with open arms had he shown up at her door and she absolutely believed getting him back was the only way she would heal. She said, 'I'm dying inside because I miss him so desperately.' When a person is in deep denial like this, it's very difficult, if not impossible, to help them to recover. The first rule of recovery is you have to be ready to heal. You have to have reached your own rock bottom and know you've had enough, and the time has come.

Narcissists will even try to take your children from you, in many cases they have succeeded. Some have resorted to false allegations of child abuse, molestation and drug-taking to persuade the authorities the parent was unfit to be in the children's lives. Unfortunately, the legal system is still pretty much clueless about the ability of narcissists to deceive and manipulate. Given their ability to come across as charming, charismatic and fine, upstanding pillars of the community, they easily convince the powers-that-be of their suitability as the better parent. On the opposite end, the other parent has been systematically abused, traumatized and is unable to mount a defense strong enough to beat the narcissist. And of course, finding a lawyer who knows anything about narcissistic abuse is very difficult. It is unfathomable to a normal person how anyone could want to try to take children away from a parent and the lengths they will go to to achieve their selfish aims. It makes my blood boil with indignation, so I can only imagine the suffering it causes the one it's happening to.

The truth is, if you are an Empath/HSP, your greatest strengths are your greatest weaknesses when you come into contact with a narcissist and you, more than anyone, need to be aware and alert so that you can protect yourself from these vile predators.

10. Empaths are sometimes Codependent

These two terms are often confused. I want to make it clear that I've said 'sometimes' because not ALL Empaths are codependent. Codependency is defined as:

'a person with an excessive emotional or psychological reliance on a partner, typically one who requires support on account of an illness or addiction.'

If you grow up with a dysfunctional parent(s) you often become the parent. I have heard it from many women that they had to 'mother' their mother'. In order to please your parent, you put their needs first and learned to ignore your own. You also develop a distorted sense of your own worth because this is the only way you get to feel needed. Such an upbringing creates codependency and you may not even be aware of it.

This is delightful for narcissists because codependents are typically drawn into relationships that are emotionally disastrous because they are unable to sustain healthy, fulfilling relationships and they are constantly seeking validation from outside of themselves. They don't believe that they DESERVE anything better. Codependents are People-Pleasers in the extreme. They will sacrifice themselves in every way to please the narcissist. Combine the Empath's traits with codependency and you have the narcissist's dream. You will also often find narcissists who have alcohol or drug addiction, making a bad situation immeasurably worse

This is deadly for you because this pattern will repeat itself in your adult relationships and you become the enabler for the narcissist. Toxic relationships need two people for them to work. Your subconscious programming will ensure your need to feel needed is met, even while it works to destroy you. Over time in a toxic relationship, your **sense** of self becomes more and more reliant on the narcissist's opinion of you. Can you see how easy it will be for them to crush what little self-worth you had to start with?

The truth is, if you suspect that you have codependency issues and you are an empath or HSP, you should consider getting a therapist who will be able to help you understand why you've become codependent and help you become aligned with your true self.

What can you do? My advice

Since this flag is not a 'trap' in the way the others are, you can't 'avoid' it in the same way. However, I want to share with you what I believe is the most important thing that you can do, and indeed should be doing, every single day to protect yourself from negative energy. I learned all about psychic protection, sacred space clearing, Chakra alignment, auric field energy, Kirlian Photography and Reiki in my early 30s when I first got into the healing field. I used to regularly attend 'Mind, Body, Spirit' seminars and psychic fairs in London. As I was regularly seeing clients at my clinic in Covent Garden, it was important that I did not get sucked into the vortex of other people's emotions. Two techniques I used after every client were 'White Light' protection and 'Space Clearing.'

White Light Protection Meditation

This technique is simple but powerful and is used by psychics, mediums, Lightworkers, healers and therapists like myself all over the world, to protect our 'energy field' and keep out negative energy. I've been doing it ever since I learned it, and I teach it to all my clients. You simply sit quietly with your feet on the ground, back straight, hands in your lap or by your side (alternatively, you can also do this lying down in bed) and imagine a powerful beam of white light is coming out of the sky and beaming down on you. Imagine the light honing right in on your heart and then spreading through your whole body.

Now imagine it spreading out around you. Your auric field extends approximately as wide/far as your outstretched arms. Stretch your arms out to your sides, upwards, above your head, in front of you and behind you. This is the area your aura takes up, so when you're working with the white light let it fill the area around you to this size. If you believe in a higher power or source that feels good to you, imagine the light is coming from that source. Let the light flood you and bask in it for a few minutes. Imagine you have an invisible zip you can circle round your aura to keep this protective shield in place. Do this technique every morning or evening, or both.

Space Clearing

If you know anything about space clearing, you'll probably think you need to be burning sage all the time. Whilst sage is indeed a great space-cleansing tool, it's not essential. There are two much simpler ways you can do it and these (among many others), I learned from bestselling author and spiritual teacher, Denise Lynn, during one of her seminars I attended in London many years ago. One is to use a bell, the other is to just 'clap it out' using your hands. If you've had an argument or whatever with your partner, do this exercise as soon as that person has left the room. Open the windows if there are any, if not, open the door of the room – negative energy needs a quick path out of your house. If you have a small bell, 'walk' the area where the argument happened, going in a clockwise direction and ring the bell every few seconds as you do so.

If you don't have a bell, clap your hands quickly 3 times as you 'walk' the area. This simple technique will clear the negative energy from the room. You can do this even if there was no argument – perhaps you were given the Silent Treatment and you can still feel the weight of that even though your partner has left. Clap or ring it out. You will FEEL the difference when you do this. If you have time and want to make yourself feel better still, light scented candles or add some uplifting essential oils to a burner. Then if possible, sit for a few minutes and do the 'White Light' meditation too.

I sincerely hope this section has helped you to more clearly see and understand the potential dynamics and interplay between empaths/HSPs and narcissists. If you are not using any kind of 'protection', please start doing those two. They will help you! Don't let those beautiful traits that make you YOU be exploited.

Knowledge is power and working with energy in this way is more powerful than you can imagine.

Flag No 15: You had an abusive childhood, or have narcissistic parent(s)

In the same way as I said being an Empath/HSP makes YOU a Red Flag, so does this one. This, more than any other, makes you a highly vulnerable target for narcissists because they not only know how to find your weak spots, they know how to exploit them. Keep in mind what I said in Red Flag No 6; they may already know, having gleaned the information from your unsuspecting friends, that you've had a hard life or have dysfunctional parents.

If you've been unfortunate enough to have a narcissistic parent, this massively predisposes you to attracting more narcissists later in life. You'll attract partner after partner, spouse after spouse (one client of mine is in the process of divorcing her fourth narcissist), you'll be emotionally wrung out, depressed, confused and you won't understand why this keeps happening to you. There is a very valid reason why this happens.

Children learn from their parents. When you are constantly being invalidated, mistreated and do not have your emotional needs met, your normal childhood developmental process is thwarted. You develop your own representation of 'normal' based on constantly trying to behave in a way that pleases your narcissistic parent but no matter what you do, you can never get it right. The nature of a narcissist is such that they don't want you to. They want to keep finding reasons to criticize and chastise you. They don't love and praise you for milestones at school, don't allow you to express yourself, think for yourself or have your own opinions or feelings. Growing up in this kind of abusive environment teaches a child that they don't matter; they exist only as an extension of their parent.

If you've been brought up in a 'Toxic Trio' situation of domestic abuse, mental ill-health and substance misuse, you are at significant risk. According to the NSPCC Domestic Abuse facts and Statistics (UK) report in June 2017, around 1 in 5 children have been exposed to domestic abuse and are more likely to have behavioral and emotional problems. For such children, growing into healthy individuals with solid self-esteem is not easily accomplished.

Children in abusive situations constantly try to think ahead to behave in a way which will cause less friction and this is what leads to them becoming 'People Pleasers'. In some cases, they go the other way and become totally rebellious and start acting out, getting into drugs and alcohol or other risky behavior and many of them marry to escape their parents, only to find themselves in exactly the same kind of abusive situation with their spouse.

What happens here, put very simply, is when you've been shaped by observing dysfunctional parents, you consider this normal and your behavior is based on what you've learned watching them. In cases where let's say, your father was abusive and your mother was submissive and abused herself, you'll learn that women can't or don't stand up for themselves. How can you possibly grow up to know what a healthy relationship looks like when you've had role models who are screwed up themselves?

Often, you wouldn't have realized that you were in an abusive relationship until you were much older. You could have been in your 20s or your 60s before the penny finally dropped and you realized that YOU were never the problem - all your problems now are due to having a NPD mother or father.

It's bad enough to have any narcissist in your life, but having a narcissistic mother is probably the toughest of all for a woman. Why? Because typically mothers are supposed to be loving, caring, nurturing, protective, supportive... all those things your Narc mother wasn't. That loving mother-daughter bond just wasn't there and this creates a huge deficit of self-love in you. The one person in the world who was supposed to love and protect you – didn't.

Also, in these cases, if the father is present, even if he has tried to be a good guy to you, his influence on your emotional wellbeing is negligible and that's because negative input into our mind is more powerful than positive in such situations. Your father's attempts to be kind and supportive would not have negated your mother's constant barrage of negativity. You can also feel a deep sense of betrayal because your father failed to protect you. In cases where there is a very domineering, narcissistic mother, the father if he is not abusive, is weak himself and lacks the character and mettle necessary to stand up to his abusive wife. He is also a victim, so neither parent provides a healthy role model for the child.

When you were growing up, your emotional needs were never met, but on top of that, you may have gotten used to hearing horrendously hurtful words from your mother. She may have said things to you such as:

'I wish you'd never been born'
"Having you ruined my figure'
'You're just a burden to me'
"You spoiled my chances of... blah blah...'

Consider the impact of such words on a child. Imagine saying those kinds of things to a child you know or to your own child or even to an adult. How would that make anyone feel?

If your mother or father treated you like this, they probably also ruined every special event you ever had, made everything in life about them, and you would have felt like a burden for just being alive. You were a mini-slave, running, fetching and carrying and doing stuff at their behest, taking care of them when they should have been taking care of YOU, and all their problems would have been YOUR fault. They communicated in their actions you were to blame for everything.

So, assuming you've grown up in this toxic childhood, your worldview will be very different from someone who's grown up in a 'normal' household. You've been denied the all-important bonding and love that is every child's right. It's one of the reasons I use Inner Child healing as part of my therapy with all my clients because it's incredibly powerful and so desperately needed.

But what if you had a happy childhood?

It is also possible you had a happy childhood, with perfectly nice, good parents, but something could have happened when you were very young which had a hugely negative image on your self-worth. I want to share an example that happened to one of my clients, who had been through four narcissistic marriages by the time she came to me and she was in her early 60s. When we started looking into what had caused her the most emotional pain, this is what emerged:

She was 8 years old and in school one day she drew 'A real pretty picture' for her teacher and left it on her desk during recess. When class resumed, the teacher saw the drawing and held it up. 'Who drew this?' she asked. My little 8-year-old client was too shy to speak or put her hand up, but she felt proud to see the teacher holding her drawing. Then, when nobody spoke, and with a look of annoyance on her face, the teacher crumpled the drawing up into a ball and tossed it in the wastepaper basket.

This cruel, thoughtless act by an adult who should have known WAY better, crushed the little 8-year-old child and created a deep emotional wound that would still be hurting my client, more than 50 years later. She broke down in tears as she remembered the story and I was able to explain to her time is irrelevant to your subconscious – when something deeply hurts you, it lodges there in a way which is timeless, it is always there underneath the surface. The message to an innocent 8-year-old child old was loud and clear. This drawing is rubbish. A child translates that into: 'You are rubbish!' What also happens then is when other incidences occur making you feel inadequate, they get added on top of this old wound and reinforce the belief that you are not good enough. That pain will only go away once it has been reframed and the Inner Child healed.

Of course one single incident like this will not be enough to cause emotional catastrophe, but those seeds of doubt, once sown, can continue to grow into a deep wound that festers away inside you. Perhaps you were bullied at school because you were clever, or different. School bullying is another form of very damaging abuse. Or there could be other reasons why you learned to be fearful and have very little confidence in yourself, and the world didn't feel like a safe place for you. There are many root causes for our emotional wounds.

When you then become involved with a narcissist, they are adept at finding those wounds and brainwashing you, using a variety of techniques covered in this book. Most pointedly, they erode your sense of self so systematically over time, you forget who you really are. All those deep-seated doubts about your own self-worth get played on and you're reminded of your own worthlessness. You always bring it back to you, to your inadequacies, but the truth is, it's not you. It's them twisting your reality, every time.

If you had a very loving, happy childhood you could have grown up trusting everyone, because you believe that the world is a reflection of what you know, and all people are good. You have had no experience of toxic, evil people, so you don't even know that such people exist in the real world. Being open and trusting can also make you very easy prey for a narcissist. Your worldly naivety makes you vulnerable.

Coming back to the Red Flags… having grown up in a toxic environment, or for whatever reason, believing you don't matter and you are worthless, you're desperately seeking love because deep down, your Inner Child is craving the love it never got. This is a need you are not even aware of, but the Romantic Predator can sense it. Combine this with your Empathetic nature, learned codependency and inability to love and validate yourself, and you become the perfect target for a narcissist. At a subconscious level, there is a familiarity about this type of controlling person that causes you to gravitate to them. It's a complicated dynamic you don't even realize is happening.

How to avoid the trap – my advice

As I mentioned in the empath section, 'Know Thyself'! You need to know your weaknesses and start working on healing yourself. This is by no means a five-minute fix because healing yourself at a deep level takes time, self-reflection, introspection, self-analysis, courage, willingness to face your painful past and ultimately a powerful desire to truly heal and recover. There is so much to be said about healing I can't cover it all here. I'm going to be going deep into healing in my next book.

For now, understand loving yourself first and foremost is where you need to focus. Again, this ties in with Inner Child healing. It's where the love is… all the love you could possibly ever want or need, is hiding inside you. It's where healing truly begins. You just need to realize it, and when you do, the love floodgates will open for you. I've seen it happen time and time again with my clients. You become that bird who flies free of the cage at last… free and flying into the light.

I also recommend getting a therapist. Of course, I would, I'm a therapist myself! But seriously, one of the best investments you can ever make in yourself is to find a good therapist who understands

NPD and abuse. A therapist can help you to sort through the emotional quagmire much faster than if you try to go it alone. In the meantime, learn all the flags in this book and if you keep them in mind, you will be well armed against any future Narc Attack that might come your way.

Red flag No 16: You're my Soul Mate. It's destiny!

This is closely linked to Red Flag No 14, because when they trot this one out, you're going to be much more vulnerable and inclined to believe it simply because you're an Empath and this fits into your thinking. Because Narcissists typically 'target' Empaths/HSP, they know your personality type and they know you believe in higher powers, destiny, Twin Flames and Soul Mates. If you believe in other spiritual entities – e.g., Guardian Angels, Starseeds, Lightworkers or the Zodiac, they will be 'into' all this too, and will waste no time in telling you that you are their Soul Mate and that Destiny has brought you together at last.

Even if you're not an Empath or HSP, the chances are you're a very nice, kind, decent person who only wants to make the world a better place. You're typically understanding, forgiving and willing to give a new relationship everything you've got. Unfortunately, all of these qualities make you a prime target for a narcissist , as I've explained in Red Flag No 13. They are looking for someone like you, someone who has all these great qualities, they know they can use them to emotionally manipulate you, and to eventually destroy you.

How to avoid the trap – my advice

Here are a few tips to help you to protect yourself.

Test the waters

The minute you meet someone who seems to 'get' this whole 'spiritual' side of you, mentally step back and ask yourself if this is possibly a ruse. Probe a little, talk a bit about the more obscure aspects of your spiritual beliefs. Ask them (for example) what their Starseed Awakening was like. Ask them if they feel that innate longing to return home. Ask them who is their favorite author in this field. See what else they seem to know about your subject. Quite often their knowledge will be very superficial (unless they are Cerebrals – they may be able to converse easily on any given subject) and you can find this out pretty quickly. If this happens, file it under Flag. If they seem genuinely very knowledgeable, be even more suspicious because it could mean they have done a LOT of research and really want to hook you.

Boundaries again

It's vitally important you set your boundaries with a set of 'Deal Breakers' you are absolutely not willing to compromise on for anyone.

Know the Flags

Read over all the Flags and be very familiar with them so you recognize them as potential flags when they show up. You'll be surprised how quickly your antenna goes up once you know what to look out for.

Know thyself

Know that as an Empath/HSP you are much more vulnerable and work at creating those boundaries and protective measures to keep the negative energy out of your world. I'm a great believer and regular user of meditating on white light/healing energy as a form of psychic protection. I recommend you make this part of your daily self-care ritual.

Red Flag No 17: They want to meet your family/friends BUT their family is a different story

Family

Most people, when they start dating, want to get to know a bit about the person first, before they even think about introducing them to friends and then family. If this person is the charming, good-looking type, their agenda is usually to meet and charm all your friends and family and convince them they are Mr./Ms. Wonderful.

This is often a ploy to get on your family's good side and turn them against you when they get to the devaluing and discarding stage. They're so good at faking the charm, they get away with this ruse. You might find this unbelievable, but I hear it all the time. Narcissists turn your family and even best friends against you - they're that good at subterfuge, character assassination and manipulating the people you love, as well as manipulating you. The vulnerable narcissists also know their shy, unassuming character can be very endearing to your folks, and they will likely take to them quite quickly.

Friends

Whenever you've got a new romantic interest in your life, of course you want to share the good news with your friends. That's what we do. The narcissist will be very keen to meet your friends as soon as possible, under the ongoing love bombing guise of wanting to know and share everything in your life; the truth is far more sinister. They want to meet them so they can gauge where they might fit into the narcissist's overall plan for you. Will they be enemies or allies when the time comes to devalue and discard you? Their hidden agenda may include assessing your friends to evaluate them as to their:

1. Potential new supply (countless new affairs start this way)
2. Potential supplementary (secondary) supply

3. Loyalty to you – how likely are they to turn against you and believe the narcissist's lies
4. Potential for triangulation and becoming flying monkeys (Red Flag Nos 38 and 46)
5. Ability to see through them and dislike them – which means these friends will need to be isolated from your life.

All of these happen every day. Friendships are shattered because of the narcissist's need to gratify his/her need for 'fuel' at any cost. And it always costs YOU.

How to avoid the trap – my advice

Family

Don't be pushed into letting them meet your family until you are ready and feel you really know them well enough now. If they keep bringing it up, saying things like 'Oh but I just want to meet the wonderful people who brought you into this world' or some such flowery nonsense (because that's what it is, let's face it!), be wary. Why are they so keen to do this, when they're only just getting to know you? Ask yourself that question and make a mental note of how often it comes up. If it comes up early and often, file it under flag!

Friends

I think it's unrealistic to not let them meet your friends, but of course, the glaring flaw here is that they'll charm your friends the way they've charmed you, so this is not going to help. In fact, it often makes things worse because it will be harder for your friends to believe you when you try telling them the truth. It's also going to be very difficult to avoid them meeting your friends, because they will want to introduce you to all theirs, they'll be all over SM sharing you, posting pictures of your new relationship together and praising you to high Heaven. But, therein lies another Red Flag, No 19, coming up shortly.

There IS a way to protect yourself from this. Confide in someone you can trust and tell them about any potential flags you have identified – **do this EARLY on and BEFORE you introduce** the new BF/GF to anyone. Keep this friend/family member posted on new developments. This is invaluable because your friend or family member won't be besotted with the person the way you are and they can be more objective when they do finally meet them. They are also going to be far more likely to believe you when the inevitable downfall comes and the narcissist starts smearing you to all and sundry because you've warned them about your concerns early on.

An absolutely critical piece of advice I want to share here is this: NEVER abandon your trusted friends in favor of a romantic partner. Nobody who has your best interests at heart would ever want to separate you from your friends so if this person is trying to do that, think about it carefully and stand by your friends. The time will come when you will need them and they will be your port in a very big, nasty storm.

You want to be in control, so, head them off at the pass and don't let them railroad you into meeting everyone in your life until YOU feel ready to and then take it gently. Introduce them to a couple of trusted friends (the one above lol!) or double date with a friend of yours so that you can get your friend's opinion. Take it slowly and keep watching for the signs. Sometimes people can see things in a person that you can't so it will be interesting for you to hear what your forewarned friend will think. Don't be surprised if they think this person, having been on his/her best behavior, 'seems lovely'. Keep reporting the flags to them. Don't let yourself be swayed into thinking that they ARE truly wonderful until you know for sure they are.

And also consider the specialist groups in Facebook where you can share your concerns and potential flags there. I have groups for both men and women and I'll put the links at the end of the book.

Their Family is a different story

When it comes to their family however, it's a different story. They have fractured, or no, family connections. They will say they have no contact with their family, refuse to talk about them at all, give vague or evasive answers or say they're dead. They'll often make it very clear the first time you ask that they don't want to discuss their family. Similarly, when you ask or talk about childhood memories, they'll say they can't remember or there wasn't anything special about it.

Vulnerable narcissists may tell you they had abusive or cruel parents whom they never see and on whom they blame everything. This plays the victim card nicely and pushes your empathy/caring/healing buttons. You'll want to help heal them because you're an Empath. Don't fall for it. They are playing you.

Another common one is if they have a parent, usually it's their mother or possibly a sibling, who dotes on them and thinks the sun rises and sets with them. This could be an indication that they are the 'Golden Child', in this case they could commit bloody murder right in front of their mother's eyes and she'd help them bury the body, so when it comes to the Devaluing, Discarding and Smear Campaigns, you'll be facing the mother's wrath as well.

Or you could find yourself in a situation like one of the guys in my Facebook Men's Group. His girlfriend and his mother are narcissists and he's shared with me some of the vitriolic texts that the mother has sent to him. He's being emotionally and financially abused to the degree that they have him almost convinced that he is Bipolar and he's about to start taking medication for a condition he doesn't even have. These people are without conscience and are dangerous to your emotional and physical health. Make no mistake about it, either scenario is BIG Red Flag.

How to avoid the trap - my advice

If they don't appear to have 'normal' family relationships and by now you've also identified several other potential Red Flags, file this one under flags too. I'm very aware of the fact that if you have not had a normal upbringing yourself, dysfunctional families may actually seem normal to you because you don't have any other point of reference to go on. This is why it's so important to 'Know Thyself' and understand your difficult childhood makes you more vulnerable. As I've explained in Red Flag No 15, if you're seeing signs of a dysfunctional family in this person, you must NOT ignore this particular Flag.

If their mother adores them or you observe a very close family pairing that seems off from the first time you meet them, get the hell out of there as fast as you possibly can.

Red Flag No 18: They have no solid/long-term friendships

If you look closer at their circle of friends and do a little bit of subtle detective work, you'll discover they have no longstanding friendships and most, if not all of the people they will introduce you to will be superficial, 'Fair-weather' friends or even casual acquaintances. These 'friends' are very likely to be under the spell of the fake persona the narcissist has shown them, so none of them will know the truth about this person. They will believe all the glowing surface traits: this person is wonderful, kind, smart, decent, fun. Aren't you the lucky one! Oh boy.

Unless they are part of what HG Tudor calls 'Lieutenants' 'which I've mentioned in Red Flag No 6. These creeps know exactly what is going on and they will eventually become the flying monkeys who will join the smear campaign fray against you when the discard comes. I'll go into flying monkeys and smear campaigns later on.

How to avoid the trap – my advice

Do not trust ANY of their friends. Keep conversations neutral and as bland as possible. Realize anything you say to them (because you don't know who is an ally and who is not) will get back to the narcissist. Also avoid becoming friends with them on SM. Giving them friend access lets them into your world where they can spy on you, and when the discard comes, they can do plenty of damage before you've had time to block them. Keep them all out of your SM.

If they ask you to accept them, or why you haven't already, this will put you on the spot, so be ready for it. Just joke and say, 'I never add people unless I've known them for at least 5 years!' Practice this a few times in the mirror at home so that it comes out of your mouth easily. If they ask with genuine concern or interest 'Oh, why's that then?' again, keep it light. Say something like 'Oh it gets so difficult to keep up, so I don't bother.' And leave it at that. Remember you do not owe this person any explanation or access to your life you are not ready to grant. Change the subject. And in your mind, picture a big flying monkey, and file this friend under Flags too.

Red Flag No 19: They want to share you with the world

They will be very eager to introduce you to all their friends initially, (on Social Media and in person) and they'll gush about how amazing you are and how lucky they are to have met you and so on. They'll plaster the pair of you all over SM and you'll feel so happy and excited because surely, if they are showing you to the world in this way, they must really be in love with you, right? Wrong. They are doing this for a whole different set of reasons than what you think.

They want to keep you besotted, and they want you to think they are besotted with you, but they are also staking their claim to you for the entire world to see, so it's clear that you're now off the market and you *belong* to them. You'll see this public adoration and display of love as enthralling, but the nefarious undercurrent is what you really need to be aware of.

How to avoid the trap – my advice

In these early days, back in Flag No 3, I advised you NOT to add them to your SM but let's assume you did anyway. It happens. I understand! But now you need to use your head and think. Why the rush and the push to get you embroiled in their world so quickly? What's the big hurry here? Ask yourself these questions.

If they do this very early on, you need to picture that HUGE Red Flag blowing wildly in the wind. And get your head back into 'normal'. Normal people do NOT do this the minute they start dating someone or even once they've been dating for a while. Sure, they might share a picture here and there or showcase a special occasion, but with the narcissist, it's like every day is a big special occasion. Ask yourself why would they do this? What's this all about? Why are they parading you on SM like they've just won the Lottery? Are you being objectified like a flashy new car or yacht? The answer to that one is yes, you are. It's another Red Flag to add to your list.

CHAPTER THREE

GETTING DEEPER INTO THE RELATIONSHIP: THE CRACKS BEGIN TO SHOW
RED FLAG Nos 20-26

Now let's say they've passed the initial stages, enough for you to give them the benefit of the doubt and you've had a few more dates with them. They've been on their best behavior, adoring you like no one ever has before, and making you walk up there on cloud nine every minute of the day. You're head over heels in love and now the relationship is FULL on. You're in! You will have ignored several Red Flags; I know you will - because narcissistic seduction is THAT powerful. No matter how many warnings you've felt, the sexual/emotional pull was just too strong to ignore. You just couldn't resist and you couldn't help yourself. Ironically, that powerful feeling, that pull, that is so beautiful now will be what comes back to haunt you in the future and keep you imprisoned in a relationship with a person who is pathologically wired to destroy you.

But for now, it's all sunshine and roses. How long this 'honeymoon' aka 'Love Bombing' stage goes on varies from one narcissist to the next. It could be a matter of weeks, months, or even years.

But hang on, because you're not out of the woods yet. You need to remain in detective mode until you can really be sure that have passed all your tests with flying colors as you progress deeper into the relationship. In addition to keeping an eye out for all the flags just covered, there are a whole lot of new Red Flags that can show up during this phase, so let's have a look at those now.

Red Flag No 20: They want to move in with you, marry you and get pregnant

Some Romantic Predators are not afraid of 'commitment'. Quite the opposite. They start talking about moving in together, marriage and having babies way too soon! If they are doing this, don't just be wary – get out! Don't mistake these ploys as 'proof' they must love you if they want to spend the rest of their lives with you and have children with you. That's not why they are doing it and you absolutely must wake up if this is happening and understand what is really going on in their heads. Narcissists do this because they want to secure you as a long-term supply of fuel. And when they ask you to commit to them in this way, have determined that you are an excellent source of narcissistic supply and you are going to suffer more emotional damage than you can possibly imagine.

Let's have a look at these scenarios individually because they are all huge Red Flags that you need to be aware of.

They want to move in with you

This will be very tempting for you because you'll see it as a sign they are serious about you and the relationship. They must be really in love with you, right? This makes you feel so good and it strengthens the growing bond you have with them. You'll feel overjoyed they want to make this commitment and take the relationship to the next level.

STOP! Their reasons for wanting to move in with you are far more sinister. Moving in with you provides them with a host of benefits which haven't even crossed your mind at this stage. Here are the main ones:

Snooping

By living in your place, they can find out more about you. When you're not around, they have unfettered access to snoop through all your personal items and will read your diaries, old love letters, access your computer (they will casually hover over you when you go to log in to your Laptop and they'll memorize your password – easily done as they'll touch your shoulders, kiss the top of your head or murmur some endearment into your ear, thereby distracting you from the fact that you are typing in your password and they can see it). What they learn about you gives them more power and control over you. And you don't even know it.

It's cheap!

Another reason is by living with you, they don't need to pay rent, utilities, etc., and I go into this in more detail in Red Flag No 25, They Financially Abuse you. At this point, you'll have no idea you are dealing with a relentless freeloader. They might help out around the house and buy a few gifts for your home initially and such actions lull you into a false sense of security. But it won't last long.

You're the Caregiver

In no time, you'll be doing their washing, ironing, cleaning the house, cooking and they will be too busy or tied up to help with such menial tasks. If you're dealing with the vulnerable narcissist – who's ultra-likely to be the one pushing you in this category - they'll be feeling too tired or too unwell and you'll just slide into permanent 'Caregiver' mode and do the work because it's what you do... just as if you were looking after children.

They can flee whenever they want to

Many narcissists (particularly the 'Elites') keep their own homes (which you may never or rarely, get to see). They do this so they can flee whenever they want or need to. They will usually do their disappearing acts during the devaluing stage when they want to punish you and they need to have their own escape pod for this. Also, when they want to discard you, it's easy to just toddle on back to their own place and forget all about you.

How to avoid the trap – My advice

You already know what I'm going to say here, don't you? By now you should be catching on! Do not move in with this person if they are pushing you to in the early days. Moving in with a new person is a big commitment and you should only do it if you are really sure you know the person well enough. If you've identified lots of Red Flags by now, go back over them all carefully and listen to your gut. If there are a bunch of them on your list by now, it goes without saying you should not be thinking of getting deeper into the relationship by moving in with them or moving them in with you. Don't be rushed or pushed into living with someone. Take your time or you will be very sorry.

They want to marry you, or get pregnant

These are the big guns of the Romantic Predator. Because both signify a lifetime commitment. This is the stuff of serious relationships, right? So why would anyone suggest marriage and children if they weren't serious? It's because if they can bind you emotionally, financially and legally to them, it makes it much harder for you to break free of them and when you do wake up and decide to divorce them, watch out because you are in for absolute hell.

If you're a woman dating a guy, then he will talk about how much he wants children, and specifically, how much he wants YOUR children. This is a powerful emotional pull for any woman who dearly longs for a baby. How do you resist a man you're in love with and who wants your baby? If you're a man dating a female narcissist, you can easily find yourself with a pregnant girlfriend. I don't need to explain how!

'Why' is the question you might be asking. Why would they do this? They do this to bind you to them and keep you (and any children who are born) as supply. This sounds callous and offensive even as I type it, but it's the raw, horrible truth. They do not love or care for you or the children. They only see you as a means of supplying them with fuel.

How to avoid the trap – my advice

Be highly suspicious of early desire to marry you or have children with you. Getting to this stage in any normal relationship takes time and suggesting it after only knowing you a few weeks or months is just NOT normal. Ask yourself why is this person in such a rush? What's the hurry? Get your head out of the clouds and put your ego in a box. This is not realistic! Tune into yourself and listen to those warning bells. Trust your gut that deep down is telling you what you already know. Do not fall for it, do not agree to get married or pregnant. If you already have children, they may well say they want to legally adopt them. This can be a very powerful motivator to con you into believing they are in it for the long haul, that they want you and your children to be safe, secure and happy. Do not fall for it. If they get legal rights to anything in your life, your precious children included, this will make it much more difficult to untangle yourself from them in the end.

When you refuse any of these big enticements, watch for their reactions, because that's going to give you another indication you are dealing with a narcissist. If you're dealing with the Vulnerable type, they will act hurt and upset that you don't love them the way they love you and they will very possibly go into a sulk and behave rather childishly.

If you're dealing with the more accomplished Covert, they will feign understanding and say, 'Of course! We need more time! It's just that I am so in love with you, I can't imagine spending my life with anyone else! I can't stop imagining our beautiful children!' Or some such flowery nonsense designed to keep pushing your emotional buttons. Such talk will make you feel that you are not giving enough to the relationship and this puts subtle pressure on you to give in.

Another ploy they will use is to hint, very subtly and kindly, that they don't know if they can risk being with a woman who is not prepared to make this long-term commitment to them. This plays into a well-known psychological sales tactic, 'Fear of Loss'. If we fear we are going to lose something, we want it more, we want it now and we'll do whatever it takes to get it. The narcissist knows this, so this subtle implication they might leave you if you don't marry them or agree to get pregnant will cause you to comply. You won't even realize you've been manipulated because it's been done so subtly.

Understand these tactics and don't be fooled by them. If they start happening, see them for what they are – Red Flags of the romantic predator, and get out of the relationship. I know I keep saying that, but it's the only way to protect yourself.

Red Flag No 21: They have a sense of entitlement/self-Importance

These two are on the list of 9 Traits outlined in the DSM-5: 'Have a sense of entitlement and require constant, excessive admiration' and 'Have an exaggerated sense of self-importance'. Have you noticed these showing up? It's easy to miss in the early days because you're in love and you know how love is blind, right? You overlook or just don't see the obvious. Often, it's other people who see this and point it out. You'll still choose to ignore it or overlook it because you want to see the best in them and your heart is desperate to believe this person is 'The One'. But as time goes on, these traits start to show up more and more as the initial sheen starts to wear off. A narcissist cannot keep their fake persona on display all they time. The truth of who they are invariably starts showing through.

They expect you to be available constantly to meet their needs but yours are totally unmet and never important. These traits begin to pervade every aspect of their behavior and their relationship with you. You'll start putting aside your basic needs in favor of meeting theirs.

This sense of self-importance is often displayed in their obvious vanity, particularly the somatic narcissist. You might notice their love of mirrors and their own reflection – they can't walk past a mirror or shop window without checking themselves out. They are self-absorbed and always fishing for compliments. They spend hours in the bathroom getting ready every day. You're already beginning to feel a sense of unease deep down, that this person is not who or what you thought they were.

How to avoid the trap – my advice

Listen to your heart at this point because these feelings are trying to warn you and if you don't listen, you are just setting yourself up for unbelievable emotional (and possibly sexual, physical and financial) abuse.

If this person seems to think they have a right to everything without question, start writing it all down. Putting pen to paper takes the guesswork out of it. Now ask yourself what was wrong with a situation that happened with them? Why didn't it feel right? What would you have done or said in the same situation? Is there a pattern of entitlement showing up? Does this person consider what YOU want or is that already starting to slip away in favor of what they want all the time?

If they exude this air of grandiosity and self-importance, add that to your journal notes too. Ask yourself overall, how is this person shaping up? Take off the blinders. Be brutally honest with yourself and listen to your gut instinct.

If you're getting yes answers to these questions, it's time to consider pulling out, especially if you have already filed several other flags. Go back and examine all the flags you've noticed and really put them under the microscope. Don't believe these are just normal 'relationship issues' that will be smoothed out over time. They won't and your suffering will get worse the longer you stay.

Red Flag No 22: They are Hyper-Sensitive to criticism and totally hypocritical

Narcissists believe they are superior to everyone else and the world should revolve around them. If it doesn't, they are likely to explode, sulk, or retaliate in some way to defend their own ideas about their entitlement to be, do and have whatever they want, when they want. It's no that they don't take kindly to criticism of any kind. Because of their own distorted view of themselves and their place in the world, you'll very soon start to realize that they can't take criticism in any shape or form.

But what is more complex and the real Red Flag here, is how they perceive criticism. You can say the most normal, ordinary thing to a narcissist and suddenly they're offended beyond all proportion to what has been said. For example, 'Honey, could you just hang the towel on the rack after your shower?' could be grounds for starting WW3.

The narcissist defines him/herself by a very flawed version of reality that is difficult for a normal person to understand, but one of the easiest ways to spot it is to just notice their behavior around simple situations in everyday life. Maybe you make a comment about something they're wearing: 'That's nice but I like the blue shirt better on you' will be translated into an insult stating you don't like what they are wearing, and you've questioned their choice. Perhaps they are watching something on TV and you suggest maybe switching channels to watch a movie, this will be seen as criticizing not only their choice of viewing, but your questioning their right to watch whatever they want will be perceived as an affront that could spark a huge row. This type of hyper-sensitive behavior will start showing up a lot and before long, you'll start feeling like you're walking on eggshells and eventually, it'll feel like you're crawling on your hands and knees over broken glass.

Sometimes, they may behave like this in front of other people when you are out and about. It's usually very embarrassing and you'll find yourself cringing, wanting the ground to open up and swallow you or mouthing apologies to people.

Totally hypocritical

In addition to the hypersensitivity, you'll also observe they are totally hypocritical when it comes to you. They can say what they like to you and about you and criticize you blatantly, even to the point of being downright nasty, using foul language and harping on you about any insecurities you've shared with them, and you'll be expected to suck it up. Yet they will drag you over hot coals and leave you smoldering in the ashes of self-doubt if they perceive the slightest infraction from you. Either way, their hypocrisy is legendary and you're the one to suffer.

Whilst they have no empathy and will hurt you and cause you pain on a daily basis, they DO feel their own pain. They feel it intensely and believe they are suffering and it's your fault. This is not only hypocritical, it's unfathomable to you. When they fear that you might leave them, they will put on a show of heartbreak, tears, the whole nine yards and you'll be so convinced that you'll forgive them because, being an Empath or a deeply caring person yourself, you can't bear to see their pain and you'll believe that they really want to change, that things will be different. But they will not. In no time at all, they will revert to their abusive type. They can't help it.

How to avoid the trap – my advice

This type of behavior is unreasonable, illogical and unacceptable. A narcissist is like a 5-year-old child. They are developmentally arrested and take that childish sense of 'Me, Me, Me!' with them into adulthood. If your partner is displaying this kind of hypersensitivity, you're in trouble. This is only going to escalate and get so much worse. If they are treating you to regular insults that leave you feeling worthless, it's time to get out.

Red Flag No 23: They are emotionally labile/volatile

In addition to this hypersensitivity, you'll soon notice your partner is emotionally labile or volatile. They have very poor self-regulation and impulse control, especially when everything in their mind doesn't work out exactly as they envision it. Their emotions are liable to change very quickly, and they blow hot and cold in the space of a few hours or in some cases, even minutes. They can burst into vicious rages, but then they fall to their knees to beg forgiveness. They are so sorry! This will never happen again! When this first happens, you will believe them. You will feel sorry for them. You will forgive them. And this will happen again and again and again.

Along these lines, you might also notice they are arrogant, rude, envious, jealous and derogatory about people. They may be very pleasant to people to their faces, but behind their backs, they say awful things about them. They are essentially two-faced in the traditional sense of the expression. You'll notice Road Rage, impatience and you'll be constantly on edge, worrying about what's going to set them off next. You end up living in a constant state of fear and hyper arousal.

To say their temperaments are mercurial is an understatement. They get bored very easily and they thrive on chaos. They are unreasonable, illogical and impossible to reason with. Living with or being with someone who behaves like this takes a serious toll on your emotional and psychological wellbeing. If you're experiencing this kind of behavior then the abuse has already begun in earnest because by accepting it, you are giving the narcissist permission to continue abusing you and that abuse is going to get a whole lot worse. Each time you forgive them, you are digging your grave deeper.

How to avoid the trap – my advice.

It is vitally important you take a good, objective look at this emotional lability. Think about what is happening to cause these emotional fluctuations or outbursts. Are they in any way relative to the reality of what has been going on? Think back over the many excuses and reasons you will have heard for the outbursts. Are they irrational? Childish? Complete fabrications of the truth? Pay attention to your own emotional balance. What is it telling you? Remember I mentioned your emotional barometer earlier on in the book? It's trying to guide you so when you think 'What the heck is going on here?' and feel utterly baffled by what they are saying, take that as a sign that this isn't normal behavior. And STOP allowing this to happen to you by leaving and going No Contact. This person is not going to change, and no amount of love from you can change or fix him/her. What more can I say?

Red Flag No 24: Work matters: They work or they don't

The reason I'm including work as a Red Flag is because with one, you're going to be doing all the work and with the other, it's important to know a polished profession or high-powered job is no guarantee a person isn't a narcissist.

The Vulnerable Narcissist

If you're dealing with a Vulnerable narcissist, they probably don't have a job and didn't when you met them. They will blame illness, injury, depression or some ailment for why they can't work. This is also a reason why they want to move in/marry you so quickly, because they want somewhere to live and someone to take care of them. You'll be the breadwinner and they will feel no obligation to contribute in any way. They will happily lie on the couch all day watching sport whilst you are at work and when you come home, they'll expect you to cook the dinner.

Your weekends will be spent shopping, cleaning, cooking and there will be no help from your partner. If you call them out on any of this, you're going to hear again about their illness, depression, or how they can't believe you'd ask them to help when you know how much they are suffering. If you do have children together, the vast majority of child-care will fall to you.

These types are lazy, work-shy hypochondriacs who will go to extremes to avoid doing anything remotely related to work. They will even fake illness and go to the Accident and Emergency at the local hospital to get checked out for some bogus complaint. Your purpose in their life is to mother them. You won't be getting any sex from them either. More on this in Flag No 35.

The Overt/Covert Narcissist

These types will have jobs because they like to be out there, meeting people, showing off their brains or bodies and especially, because they can find potential targets in and around the workplace. They may have high-powered jobs. Doctors, psychologists, pastors, lawyers, spiritual leaders, vets, professors, lecturers, teachers can all be narcissists. They are often drawn to positions of power or authority. Not surprising, they also find their way into law enforcement and military careers. They are lurking everywhere.

One of the things many narcissists in this category have in common is a very patchy job history. They will have changed jobs a lot, moved around a lot and perhaps even changed careers a lot. You'll always hear them blame the job, the boss, the team, the company – for why they left. It was never, ever their fault.

How to avoid the trap – my advice

With the Vulnerable, you can avoid the trap by talking to them about their work history and their supposed illness or whatever reason they give you for not working. How long has this been going on? Don't believe everything they tell you because they might say it's quite recent and they are keen to get back to work as soon as they are well. But that will never happen. So do some background checking of your own.

With the Overt/Coverts, a patchy career or job history is cause for concern, as is blaming everyone else for having to change jobs, so watch that one. Be aware a high-caliber job does not a high-caliber person make. Remember Flag No 2? Don't judge a book by its cover. Narcissists are hiding in plain sight everywhere.

Red Flag No 25: Prince or Pauper, they financially abuse you

This, along with sex, is one of the two biggest issues that rear their ugly heads in the world of narcissistic abuse, because a narcissist will financially destroy you. It's one of the most common complaints I hear about so I want you to pay close attention to this one so you can protect yourself from financial devastation.

The Vulnerable Narcissist (Paupers)

The Vulnerable narcissist is the Pauper who pleads poverty from the outset. They will take advantage of you as I've mentioned, because they won't work and they expect you to keep them and pay for everything. You'll be working all hours, taking care of the home, the kids and them, and they will not contribute a single cent to the household. They will spend your money as if it's their own. Even to the point of bankrupting you. If you divorce them, they'll try to take you for everything they can.

If you are the primary breadwinner and well off financially, they will spend, spend, spend all your money. This speaks to their inner core belief they are entitled to whatever they want, whether it's yours or not, including your money. Your job is to bow at the altar of their magnificence and worship at the feet of their every need. They don't care about financially milking you dry, because when they are done, they will just move on to the next wealthy person they've targeted. It happens all the time.

It's just a loan...

This is another ploy you will often hear and because narcissists are such convincing, manipulative liars, they'll convince you 'Money is coming. I'll pay you back next week/month'. But I guarantee you you'll never see a cent of the money you lend them. Do not fall for it. They'll do this even in the face of pleading poverty, and having told you they have no money, they will make up some lie about money owed to them, from some source like an old insurance policy, or a family member or some friend who owes them from way back. They may even use this 'Flying Monkey' to back up their story. Do. Not. Fall. For. This. Please!

Some may hide their true status initially or pretend to be financially well off and are generous, but this is a smokescreen and even more dangerous in the 'Loan' situation because they've led you to believe they've got money. But also be aware it's not just the vulnerable narcissist who will try to financially abuse you, as they are all quite capable of doing this, even if they are working, earning more than you, and have ample assets. None of that will matter because their goal is always to do as much damage to you as they possibly can.

I'd like to share some typical examples of how they can show up in the early days with regards to money, from feedback I've had from my group members:

The Vulnerables (Paupers)

Pleading Poverty...

"Pleading poverty, but making it look like it was a choice of lifestyle. I don't really care about fancy stuff and restaurants but he kind of hid that his finances weren't as good as he wanted them to be. Later I realized he was really stressed about money... he'd blame me for spending too much money and even convinced my mother I had a problem."

In 16 years, he never took me out...

'Very stingy from the beginning. In the 16 years he never once took me to eat out, he said he doesn't like eating in front of other people. And he never took me anywhere else. There seriously isn't one place that I can mention that he took me to. He always says people are mad to pay money to go to places when it's cheaper being at home. As for presents that was also big no-no. The only time I would maybe get something small was when he would manage to steal it somewhere. So as far as I see it Narcs hate spending money.'

Bought me a Chinese takeaway then raped me...

'Mean as hell! Bought me a Chinese take away then raped me! Told me he had been nice to me because he had bought a meal! So, thought he should have the right to sex! Next night he took a woman out to dinner! Monster!'

I loaned him $8,000...

'I loaned him $8,000 to buy a car. He worked out the monthly payments and said he could easily afford to pay me back each month from his salary. The first month came and he had some excuse and said he'd pay me the next month. 3 years on and I've not seen a penny of that money. I should have just sent him to a car dealer!'

Proposed with a ring from a bubblegum machine...

'When he proposed to me it was a ring from the bubblegum machine... and was offended when I wouldn't wear it. And when I said, "It's from the 25 cent machine!" he said, "It was actually 50 cents" ... yeahhhhhh. He did end up buying me a lot more rings and they always got nicer, but it was only an investment because when he relapsed, he would come back and take the ring to pawn it.'

The Overt/Coverts (Princes)

These are very materialistic, status-conscious and are the ones who will bombard you with gifts, expensive restaurants and trips away during the love bombing stage. They do it to impress you and get you bonded to them but they do it for other reasons too, often to impress other people or to keep up with the 'Joneses' as these examples show:

Sent flowers every day...

'Generous. Sent flowers every day for a week and a daisy to every female on my job. Insisted on our first date being Valentine's Day.'

To show what he has...

'For my Overt Narc it was always important to pay everything in restaurants and he liked making me exclusive gifts for my birthday, for Christmas and in the love bombing stage, to show what he has.'

Complained that I bought the expensive organic bananas...

'Mine always complained of needing to save money and criticized me for spending, but then always wanted to "keep up with the Joneses' and would buy all kinds of electronics and tools and always took me to extravagant restaurants and told me "I was worth it". Then the next day he'd complain that I bought the expensive organic bananas.'

If their woman looks good...

'He was generous for our entire marriage (16 years) but I think it was only to be forgiven for being so rude, mean, withholding sex and affection and/or because it looked good for him if I looked good with fine jewelry and clothes. That's all about "keeping up with the Joneses", many of them want to put on a public show and if their 'woman' looks good and has beautiful jewelry, it reflects well on them. It's always about THEM!'

When a Romantic Predator gives you a gift, there is always an agenda as I've mentioned, but what is also important to know is they will use those gifts against you further down the line. If you ever complain about them, you'll get a tirade of "After all I've done for you! After all the gifts I've bought you!' and you'll be called the most ungrateful b**** or b***ard on the planet. And one more thing, when the discard comes, they will demand all these gifts back – to sell or pawn them, as one of the examples shows. Seriously, they're that twisted.

But gifts are just one part of the ploy. Narcissists will try to get access to your bank account or they will suggest you have a joint account, and they will want to know about any assets, savings, insurance, bonds etc., you have. They will ultimately take all of it, including selling your valuables if need be (or just to spite you) and leave you in financial ruins.

There's one more situation: If you've stopped working to have children and they encourage you to stay at home, you then become financially dependent on them. This keeps more women than I care to admit stuck in abusive marriages until the children are grown up. By then, they are often depressed and suffering autoimmune diseases as a result of long-term psychological abuse.

How to avoid the trap – my advice

Observe how they are about gifts and if they start bringing or sending too many, tell them to stop, and see it as a Red Flag. Picture that bunch of roses with the yellow Narcissus in the middle – think of my book cover!

For a moment we have to put aside the issue if you have identified several Red Flags, you should not be taking the relationship any further. Because it happens, in spite of the warnings, you forge ahead with the relationship. So a golden rule in my book is to never give them access to your bank account or any of your assets, **no matter how much you think you can trust them**. Keep your own bank account separate. In fact, don't reveal anything about your financial situation to them. If they keep pushing, that is another huge Red Flag, but if you're in the relationship and believe it's for the long-term, you could agree to setting up an additional joint account that you pay X amount into to cover shared expenses but do NOT ever give up your financial independence. No matter how persuasive your partner is and they will try guilt-tripping you and use all kinds of tactics to get you to comply. Don't give in. Remember this book is about protecting yourself in the event that things DO go wrong. But even in the healthiest of relationships, I still advocate having your own money and your own separate bank account. Because even healthy relationships go wrong and you want to be used to having and managing your own finances.

And the loan Issue

In this case, instead of thinking you ought to lend them the money, ask them 'Why don't you borrow it from the bank?' or 'What are you going to do to tide yourself over?' They will likely come up with some excuses that sound plausible, but that still doesn't mean you are obliged to get them out of their financial troubles. Just say 'I can't help. I have no spare cash. It's all tied up paying my own bills.' Say this even if you DO have cash to spare. Do NOT lend it to them because if you do, you can kiss it goodbye forever.

If your partner is the Pauper, ask yourself if you're prepared to keep carrying this person financially for the rest of your life? And ask yourself why the hell should you? You've got all the right caring, nurturing instincts but you're being abused. It's time you woke up to the fact and did something about it, isn't it? If you don't they will bleed you dry of every asset you own and every cent you've earned.

And for that final situation, where you've stopped working to have children: Don't ever let yourself get into a position where you become financially dependent on your husband or the father of your children if you can possibly avoid it. This can be very difficult if you both want children and you've been persuaded to give up your job or career and you believed your partner would take care of you and the children.

If at all possible, have a savings nest egg they know nothing about, try to have a job that has Maternity Leave, and get back to work as soon as you can, even if it's only a part-time job. Bear in mind when the discard crash comes, having children with them will not suddenly make them grow a conscience where they agree to start paying child support. In more cases than I care to remember, they will not, even when court ordered to do so.

Red Flag No 26: Empty promises and 'Future Faking'

One thing narcissists are really good at is making promises they never keep. They will 'Future Fake' to get you to do what they want at any given time. This usually happens in the early stages too, but it takes on a whole new level in the relationship once you're deeper in. The promises they make initially are usually built around exciting future plans, like vacations together or even marrying you – because though many of them do want to rush you into marriage, many of them don't – but they will dangle the marriage carrot frequently to keep you hooked on the promise of this dream coming true.

They will always have excuses for delaying the plans however. They may talk excitedly about the honeymoon you'll have in the Bahamas but shut down when you try to get a date for the wedding out of them. You'll eventually get sick of hearing yourself talking like a broken record, asking them the same questions over and over and they will get irritated with you and tell you to shut up about it, for God's sake!

There are lots of other empty promises they'll make:

- Yes, we'll buy a house together
- Yes, we'll go to Paris for your Birthday
- Yes we'll move to be closer to your elderly parents
- Yes, we'll get a dog and a cat

It'll be 'Yes' to everything that excites you, but none of it will happen. And then it also starts affecting the little day-to-day things in your life.

They might promise to call you at a certain time or meet you to help with the weekly shopping, or collect something from the Dry Cleaners, or pick up a Takeaway... and turn up empty handed, then pretend they never agreed to do it in the first place. That's part of gaslighting, which I cover later.

The reason this is done is to keep you bonded to them, and keep you believing in a in a non-existent future, because they have no intention of ever keeping their word. They will lie and wriggle their way out of every promise ever made to you. If you get upset or call them out on it, they may resort to love bombing again to settle you back into trusting they really do love you and they will say they will make it up to you eventually. They never will.

This kind of manipulation is slow-burn abuse. Gradually it erodes your sense of self and those feelings of not being worthy you have been harboring deep inside are reinforced. This manipulation also leads to cognitive dissonance (Red Flag No 43) because you're struggling to reconcile the lush promises with the reality.

How to avoid the trap – my advice

Firstly, always – from the beginning - be on the lookout for a match between words and actions. Do they do what they say they will do? If you're being vigilant, you'll very quickly notice the pattern. Narcissists are notorious for saying one thing and doing another and they don't give a hoot about contradictive behavior. They don't live by the same moral code you do, so don't ever expect them to hold up their end of the bargain.

When you notice the pattern, make a note of it and ask yourself: Do you want to spend the rest of your life with a person who cannot keep their word? Is this what you signed up for? They will continue with this behavior as long as you allow it, because they can't change, but YOU can. You can call a halt to the relationship and get yourself swiftly out the door.

CHAPTER FOUR

RED FLAGS IN THE DEVALUING STAGE
RED FLAGS 27 to 40

We've covered 26 Red Flags so far and if you're still in the relationship, the worst, by far, is yet to come. Because now things start to change. They start to change because you're a normal human being and all normal human beings have flaws. When you start to question any aspect of the narcissist's behavior or personality, that worries them because there is a danger now you're going to see through them. And their anger starts to simmer beneath the surface, because you are not the perfect person they fabricated you to be and now you're daring to question them. Daring to point out *they* are not perfect. They are going to make you regret this.

They'll start devaluing you and you'll start feeling really bad. The magic slowly disappears. All the happiness and joy you felt evaporates and you realize you are feeling deeply unhappy most of the time. There will be the occasional 'Love Bomb' crumb to remind you of the 'Golden Period', but that's designed to keep you hooked (and it's the prime cause of trauma bonding, covered in a later section). Before you get to the stage of feeling totally worthless, emotionally wrung out, financially devastated and before you succumb to anxiety, depression, insomnia, C-PTSD all the many other emotional and psychological issues associated with the fallout of narcissistic abuse, there are more Red Flags that, had you known about them, might have saved you from years of heartache and pain. So, let's take a look at those now.

Red Flag No 27: They're always checking their phones/furtive with computers

They are secretive with their phone, texting a lot or walking outside to take a call, then telling you it was work or 'nothing important' when you ask about it. You will notice they never let their phone out of their sight – even taking it into the bathroom with them and sleeping with it under their pillow. You are never allowed to look at their phone. If you ever try, you'll be quickly rebuked and made to feel like a snoop.

You'll also notice similar furtive behavior with their computers or laptops. They will always have it positioned so you can't see what's on the screen, or they'll quickly change tabs or shut the lid if you approach them.

When it comes to your phone and PC, however, it's open season and remember that sense of entitlement they have wired into them? That gives them every right to not only look at your devices whenever they feel like it, but also to demand you give them your passwords. If this shocks you, trust me when I tell you I have people telling me this has happened to them regularly and they have given them the passwords. They believe they have a right to know everything going on with you, but you do not have the same rights with them. Narcissists have a keen sense of injustice to themselves, but absolutely none when it comes to you, so you will see they have two completely different yardsticks when it comes to their expectations of you and what you can expect from them. But what is far scarier is they are able to convince you they have this right, to the point you hand over your passwords and give up your right to your last shreds of privacy.

How to avoid the trap – my advice

When you notice this behavior, ask yourself the obvious question: What are they hiding? Because this behavior is indicative of nothing else. They are texting, sexting or chasing current or potential targets. Planning and scheming behind your back but often, right in front of your face. They have the gall to do this because narcissists are serial cheaters. If they're on their PC a lot, they're on dating, porn sites or communicating with various potential or current new targets or a combination of all three.

Ask yourself why they should have unfettered access to your phone / PC and even your passwords? What is going on with that? What's going on is they want to control every aspect of your life. They believe they own you and you have no right to privacy. Where is the justice or fairness in all this? The answer is: none. See this for what it is and again, ask yourself if this is acceptable to you? Are you going to put up with this for the rest of your life – or however long the relationship lasts? Because that is what they will expect.

You can try setting boundaries that they keep off your phone/PC, and NEVER give them your passwords. But seriously, do you want to be with someone who you can't trust, and who clearly, doesn't trust you? Behavior like this is disrespectful and another example of subtle abuse. These little things slowly build up until one day you will realize you have lost all control and you don't recognize yourself anymore. Get out while you still have your sanity intact.

Red Flag No 28: They're jealous and controlling

I've never liked jealousy in anyone, and have long been aware of the fact jealousy is not a sign the person 'loves you so much they can't bear the thought of anyone else looking at you', but that premise is one narcissists use so easily in the beginning, during the love bombing stage. Later on, they take it deeper and use it to emotionally blackmail you into altering your natural behavior – so effectively, you rein yourself in so as not to upset them or send them into a jealous rage. You'll start avoiding people and places where it might happen, or being much more anti-social than you normally would be so as to avoid any potential conflict. What happens is you mistake this control for love.

Jealousy has always been a sign of deep inner insecurity and nowhere does that apply more than with narcissists. They are jealous of everyone deep down, because they have no real sense of self. They 'borrow' your character in the beginning to woo you, but this false persona can't last long, and their real character starts to show through. You will see jealousy coming out of their pores, initially couched in terms of 'I love you so much, I can't stand the thought of anyone else touching you!' You hear this as love.

But it's not about love, it's about control. They show extreme jealousy because any attention you get is a threat to their status and their ego. Remember they think they own you, so no one else has any right to look at or inspect their 'property'. When the 'I love you so much...' ploy stops working, you will be blamed for inciting or encouraging the attention, regardless of how innocent you are.

But their jealousy runs far deeper than just this. They are jealous of any kind of attention, support or sympathy you get from others. If you're sick, for example (narcissists can't bear to be around sick people) they will hate that you need attention and will often find an excuse to vanish until you are back to normal or they will play down your illness and even accuse you of attention-seeking or faking it. Truly, I've heard it all.

If you consider they are jealous, suspicious and controlling because this is who they are and that's how they are wired, it makes it easier to see how they project these behaviors onto you. Their jealousy runs deep and often devolves into hatred. They hate successful people. They hate people who they see being praised at work, in sporting or social occasions. They find it difficult, if not impossible, to be happy for people.

They will be jealous of your family, friends, work colleagues and your success of any kind. They are even jealous of the attention their children get from you. How warped is that? If you're with a narcissist, you will sadly come to know just how warped their world really is.

How to avoid the trap – my advice

Such jealousy is often pathological and if you ignore the little signs in the beginning, this will allow the narcissist to take even more control. What will happen as time goes along is you will be isolated from family and friends, have no social life of your own, live under constant threat of interrogation by your partner, always have to account for every waking moment of your life, be falsely accused of cheating and be blamed for things you didn't do all the time. You will be constantly 'Walking on eggshells' or as I prefer to put it, 'Crawling on your hands and knees over broken glass'. You will at this point be deep in 'Narc Abuse Land' and your life will be a living hell.

The only way to avoid this is by taking careful stock of the Red Flags in this book as you carefully examine this person, and if you start seeing these early jealousy signs too, do NOT continue with the relationship.

Red Flag No 29: The mask is off! 8 Ways they start devaluing you

Once the initial sheen has worn off, the narcissist will start to devalue you. At this point, they no longer feel the need to pretend or hide their true self. The mask is off and now you're going to start seeing who they really are. Here's a list of some common devaluing tactics:

The Narcissist will:

1. **Criticize you** – your clothes, the way you walk, talk, eat, cook, keep house, think... nothing about you is ok anymore at this stage. They will find fault with everything.

2. **Discredit you** – nothing you've achieved will be of any value. They will constantly play up their achievements and play yours down. Nothing you've achieved has any value in their

eyes, but they will constantly play up their skills and downplay yours.

3. **Belittle you** – they'll make you feel small, inferior and worthless, by ignoring anything you say, rolling their eyes or butting in with their own glory-story because what you have to say is of no interest to them.

4. **Mock you/talk down to you** - they'll do their best to make you think you are stupid and a waste of space. Cerebrals, in particular, will use their superior intellect to make you feel stupid.

5. **Talk over you** - whether this is in private or in company, nothing you say will be heard and they will always have a bigger, better story to tell. A narcissist likes nothing more than the sound of his/her own voice and all that matters to them is what comes out of their own mouth.

6. **Bring up intimate** - or painful, personal things you've shared with them – for example, one client I worked with had shared details with her Narc about sexual abuse when she was a child. He threw this into her face several times, saying 'It's your own fault. You asked for it! You've always been a whore at heart!' Nothing is sacred and your secrets are NEVER safe with a narcissist.

7. **Compare you to others** – always negatively. They'll comment on how smart, sexy, attractive or gorgeous so-and-so is. This could be a person you both know or someone on TV. They may pull up a picture on their phone and wave it in front of your face.

8. **They glorify their Ex** – if they are not trashing their Exes, they may switch gears altogether and use their beautiful, gorgeous, wonderful Ex to batter your self-esteem. They'll

say he/she was a better cook, mother/father, lover, blah blah blah. He or she is perfection personified and you will never match up.

All of this devaluing is done to make you feel inferior, less-than and fearful of losing them to another person. And it works because it slowly erodes your self-confidence and sense of who you are. It makes you even more desperate to please them and the more you do that, the more of yourself you give up and the more they trample you into the ground.

How to avoid the trap – my advice

If you're not in a relationship now, I hope everything I've shared so far will have convinced you a narcissistic relationship is NOT where you want to be. If you're at this stage in your relationship, I have to assume you were already in the relationship by the time you picked up this book. In that case, I understand and I'm sorry. I hope what you learn here will help you better understand why you are where you are and give you the courage to start finding a way out of the relationship. Make a vow to yourself right now that you are going to get out. And find that way out, because there is a way out, and there is always light at the end of the tunnel.

My advice is to value, respect and love yourself enough to NOT accept this kind of treatment from anyone. You are worthy of love, respect, kindness and you do not DESERVE this crap. Start believing this right now and make a vow to yourself that you will never accept being treated like a doormat again.

Red Flag No 30: Gaslight-ning Strikes – and you don't know what hit you!

Gaslighting is an emotional abuse tactic used to manipulate you into questioning your own perceptions. Narcissists are adept at making you doubt your own reality.

The term originates from a 1938 play by British dramatist Patrick Hamilton. Two films were subsequently made, in 1940 and 1944, further popularizing the term. In the story, the manipulative husband keeps doing things to make his wife doubt her sanity. For example, he keeps hiding special items of hers, telling her she's to blame for losing them. She begins to think she's losing her mind and having no clue that he's the cause, she relies on him even more and begins to really believe she is mentally unwell. This is all part of the narcissist 's strategy. The gas lighting in the house keeps dimming, and she hears knocking on the walls. When she tells him, he says she's imagining it. But of course, he's responsible for both things happening, and she becomes more anxious and emotionally fragile as time goes on.

Gaslighting in today's world of narcissism is basically the same... the narcissist will keep doing and saying things to make you question your reality, refuse to admit they could possibly have got it wrong, and they are so convincing, you start really wondering if you're going out of your mind and; they are incredibly tenacious in their application of this tactic. They can keep this up endlessly, for years, if need be. They won't give up and they won't give in. You'll cave first, because nobody but a narcissist has the tenacity to keep this up. It would exhaust a normal person. That's what it does - it emotionally exhausts and weakens you.

The scary thing about gaslighting is that it's very insidious and can take many forms. For example, even if you catch them in the act of removing your things or whatever, they are so good at lying and thinking on their feet, they'll twist the reality in front of your eyes and make it something else entirely. When you try to call them out on it, they'll say you've imagined it. You've got it wrong. You're definitely losing your mind because that's not what they are doing at all. It's not what they did! It'ss not what they said! It's not what they meant! What is WRONG with you? They will lie to you - with a straight face – and even though you know it's a lie, it throws your mind into confusion because it makes no sense. They will dance around it, change the subject, give you the silent treatment, walk out of the room or the house, sulk, tell you you've got it wrong... anything but admit it was a lie. Narcissists don't do admissions of guilt, mistakes or wrongdoing. EVER.

Amid all this gaslighting, they will accuse you any or all of these things:

- Being crazy
- Needing help – you're mentally unstable
- Being jealous and insecure
- Being overly sensitive or overly reactive.
- Saying you're the problem, you need to let things go
- Saying you've got no sense of humor and can't take a joke.

They'll also deny they said or did something, even though you have concrete proof. They're so convincing in their denial you start wondering if you could be wrong. Deep down you know you're not, but because this kind of behavior makes no sense, or because you've been subjected to it as a child and consider it 'normal', you let it pass. You can catch them red-handed or in flagrante in bed with someone else, and they will twist it around and make you believe it's YOUR fault this has happened. They have even been known to say, absurdly, 'It's not what it looks like!' The hell it isn't!

There's no point in arguing with a narcissist, and you know it, because you can't win an argument. They'll start 'word-weaving' or 'word-salading' to run circles around you and you often end up not knowing what the point of the conversation was in the first place. This is further complicated when they throw in positive reinforcement during such encounters. They might pick some random compliment out of the blue, which can do any or all of three things...

1. It flatters you and reminds you of the good times and the reason why you love them

2. It reinforces your belief that of course he/she still loves you

3. It throws you completely off the scent of where you were

The more they do this, the more you become emotionally unhinged. Over time they wear you down and weaken your defenses to the point that you just don't know who you are anymore. If you're still at the stage of being in love with your Narc, a huge part of you is desperate for them to be right... so you've got this additional conflict going on deep inside. You know they're wrong, but you don't want them to be. You may even think that they ARE unbalanced and possibly mentally unstable, but because you're in love with them, that caring part of you comes to the fore... you start believing they can't help it, they don't mean it deep down. You tell yourself they really DO love you.

Being the kind, caring, empathetic person you are, your nurturing spirit kicks in and you think... and this is one of the biggest and most fatal mistakes you can ever make in a relationship with ANY narcissist ... you think you can fix them. Your love for them is strong enough to overcome any obstacle and you really believe this. When you get to this point of constantly making excuses for them or thinking you can fix them, you're on very dangerous ground indeed, because the simple truth is, you can't fix them. They don't want to be fixed, and as far as they are concerned, they're not broken.

How to avoid the trap – my advice

If you ARE being gaslighted, then what do you do about it? How do you protect yourself from this and retain your sanity? I wrote a blog about this where I shared 4 tips. They are:

Tip No 1

Everything the narcissist does is designed to undermine your sense of self, to make you feel emotionally unstable and to question who you are and what your reality is. They do this to further secure their own power. My most important advice in this is to ground yourself in reality. You KNOW you're not stupid, you know you're not losing your mind. Trust your gut! You owe it to yourself to stand firm in your belief in yourself.

Tip No 2

Next is to keep a log – and keep it in a safe place, password protected so that the narc can never access it – if you'd prefer to have a physical record, like a journal or notebook, think long and hard about where you can hide it and how accessible it will be to safely write in it. Your work desk or somewhere the Narc can't possibly access it might be best, but if that's not possible (maybe you work from home or don't work at all), you'll have to get creative about where to hide it! If your Narc is aware of it, they'll get their hands on it, read it and use it to belittle you further. Possibly (or probably) they'll even destroy it.

Jot down what's going on. Add dates, times, duration, what was said, and any other facts that emerge. Writing about it as soon as possible after the event will help you to stay grounded and know that you're not nuts. This 'dossier' may also come in very handy for you down the road when you do break free and want to remind yourself of the nightmare relationship you've escaped... this is especially useful for you when hoovering starts. It may even come in handy if you have to go to the police or you have to share some home truths with family, friends or even an attorney.

Tip No 3

Reach out to someone you can truly trust or find a support group because if you've been isolated, you may have no one to talk to (a reminder, I have two groups, one for men and one for women – I'll put the link at the end of the book) and get the help you need. Know you are not alone and you will get through this.

Tip No 4

I've said it before, and I'll say it again. Formulate an exit strategy and get out of the relationship, if you possibly can. I know there are situations where this seems impossible, and these usually involve children. Such situations are complex and require research and deep consideration. Society dictates children are better off with both parents. But if one of those parents is narcissist ic, no child is better off left in this situation. I've often heard: 'I'm staying for the sake of my children', but research shows growing up with a narcissistic parent is emotionally destructive for the child and I've outlined (Flag No 15) how that leads YOU to attracting more narcissists into your life. I acknowledge how difficult it can be, and I'm including several links in Reading and Resources Section at the end if you need to investigate this further, so you can, ultimately, make the best decision for you and your children.

But in any other situation, cut loose, go no contact and start rebuilding your life from the inside out, because you are worth it. When you know your own worth and value, it becomes much more difficult for anyone to hoodwink you. Step up for yourself. You deserve better than to be belittled, invalidated and made to feel worthless.

Red Flag No 31: Narcissists are supreme Blame-Shifters

I've lost count of the times I've heard this one from my group members. They are sick and tired of being blamed for everything going wrong in the relationship. They can do absolutely nothing right and no matter how hard they try they are still found wanting. A narcissist will blame you for things having absolutely nothing whatsoever to do with you.

- They had a bad day at work - your fault because you upset them the night before.

- They don't feel well - your fault because your cooking is terrible, you must be trying to poison them.

- They don't want to have sex with you – your fault because you've let yourself go.

These are just a few basic examples but the thing about blame shifting is it gets much more complicated than the obvious. The narcissist will use this tactic to invalidate everything about you. For example, if they upset you and you try pointing out why, they will laugh at you, dismiss it as trivial, or ridicule you. They'll trot out any number of 'classic' phrases such as:

- You're too sensitive
- You can't take a joke
- You're crazy
- Calm down
- Why is it always about YOU? (Yes, seriously, they say this!)
- You're hysterical
- You don't understand me
- I'm tired of trying to understand you

What happens then is suddenly the focus has shifted to you and it's your entire fault. And because you're often emotionally wrecked, brainwashed and traumatized by the time this starts happening, you'll turn the focus to yourself too and start thinking maybe it IS your fault after all. You're to blame. You're not, of course. It's all part of the narcissist 's plan to undermine your sense of self. Again. It's very easy for them to subtly push you from here into feeling guilty you are not giving the relationship or THEM, what they need.

And even in the cases where they cannot deny something they have said or done, they will still blame you because they can't take criticism or shame of any kind. Whatever the issue at stake is, it will be your fault because you upset them, didn't love them enough, made them unhappy, mad, sad or whatever. They will always wriggle out of it and place the blame squarely on your shoulders.

How to avoid the trap – my advice.

I've talked about grounding yourself in reality, writing things down and confiding in a trusted friend previously and those three tips come into play again here. Stop, tune into yourself, check what's going in in your body, write it all down, and call a friend to discuss it as soon as you can. Get it very clear in your head that you are not at fault and don't start accepting false blame. REFUSE!

But, don't try to get the narcissist to take responsibility and admit what they are doing. Trying to get a narcissist to take responsibility and accept blame is a total waste of your time and energy. The more you try, the more you feed their desire for fuel and the more opportunities you give them to further twist and warp the truth. This is particularly so if you are dealing with a Cerebral who will run intellectual rings around you. You will just exhaust yourself and end up more upset and shouldering the blame. Don't engage. You can win this one by exercising the three tips – grounding, writing it down and talking to a friend. Knowing this and just letting them believe have won is the best hand you can play. Whilst planning your Exit Strategy and getting out, of course!

Red Flag No 32: Projection

This is another tactic, quite similar but not the same. It's a bit more complex! Projection is an unconscious way of denying one's own feelings and attributing them to others. Because they can't deal with their own guilt or shame, they have to unleash it and you become the perfect foil.

This is when they take everything going on in their twisted minds and 'Project' it onto you. It's a different kind of blame-game. This projection can be subtle, for example in the case of the Vulnerable narcissist, they'll say you've hurt them, when it's clear they've hurt you. They will accuse you of lying, cheating, being insensitive, mean and absolutely everything they've done to you, they'll say you've done to them. You'll be reeling when you hear it because it's so absurd, you can't believe what you are hearing.

One of the reasons they are so controlling and want to monitor your phone and your every move, is because they are always up to no good, so they assume you'll be up to no good too. When you think about it, this makes total sense. They may be excellent at mimicking and mirroring other people's behavior but they have precious little understanding of real ethics, integrity and moral codes. For them, it's a defense mechanism to throw all their nefarious thinking at you because they can just offload it onto you, and that makes them feel better. If they can keep placing all the blame on you for all their s***, they'll never have to take responsibility for their actions.

They will never take responsibility because it's just not what narcissists do. They will even accuse YOU of being a narcissist and I have had plenty of women post in my group that they are worried they are narcissists themselves. I assure them if they are worried they might be, it is proof they are NOT, because genuine narcissists don't care if they are and rarely want to get help of any kind because they believe they are perfect, so why would they need help?

How to avoid the trap - my advice

See this behavior for what it is and don't buy into their false accusations, lies and attempts to paint you as the bad one. Also realize as it's a reflection of what is going on in their heads, it's giving you insight you can use to understand how their mind works. If you can take another of those 'mental steps back' I often suggest and analyze behavior from this perspective, you can get clarity on it. You can mentally deflect it by thinking 'Ah ha! He's feeling guilty about something so he's projecting it onto me!' Don't allow yourself to be unseated by things that simply aren't true. We already know trying to defend yourself is just going to get you into more complex arguments, so try Grey Rocking (more on this in Red Flag No 36). But don't agree, don't say 'Yes, ok, you're always right' because if you admit to cheating, for example, you'll never live it down. Try literally just shrugging it off saying something like 'You're entitled to your opinion' or saying you have nothing to say. And how's that Exit Plan going for you?

Red Flag No 33: They create and thrive on chaos

Life with a narcissist is never going to be peaceful and harmonious, because they get bored very easily. After the heady days of the 'Golden Period', they start to realize 'normal' is not much fun. One of my Group Members said her Ex said he missed the butterflies he'd had in the beginning of the relationship. Poor diddums! The reality is narcissists live in a fantasy world of their own making. Everyone who falls in love knows that crazy feeling of being 'in love' and totally wrapped up in this exciting new person, but over time, things settle down and as you get to know each other really well, then real love blossoms as you learn to accept each other's good and bad traits. We all have them, and we know nobody is perfect, so we learn to compromise and build a strong relationship allowing us to focus on the best parts of the person we love, whilst accepting they are not perfect.

But it doesn't work this way with narcissists. The Romantic Predator you met in the beginning has vanished and in his or her place, there is a person you barely recognize. They cannot seem to get through a single day without causing emotional chaos. Everything results in an argument, door slamming, the 'Silent Treatment' or worse. They don't want to live a normal, quiet life so they manufacture stress and strife and you're always in the firing line, you're to blame and they will make your life impossibly stressful. All of this chaos causes you to be upset and seeing you in such a state provides negative fuel for them.

What is deeply damaging is you're living in that chaos and maybe not even realizing they are the cause of your emotional state. This is because they are so good at blame-shifting, gaslighting and all their other Narc tactics, your thinking gets very foggy. Often you can't or don't connect the dots until much later on in your recovery, when the damage has been done and you are desperately trying to put the shattered pieces of yourself back together. One of my clients had a nervous breakdown and didn't realize it was caused by her Ex's gaslighting and crazy-making behavior.

How to avoid the trap – my advice

I want to remind you here this book is all about recognizing the Red Flags so you can avoid the traps in the first place; it's not a book about how to recover from narcissistic abuse – that will be my next book! If this is happening, along with a plethora of other flags, you'll at least by now know you are in an abusive relationship and my recommendation – you know it – is to get out. You will never, ever have a happy, harmonious, beautiful life with a narcissist. It will be chaos, heartache, pain and abuse all the way, and I've known people who have been stuck in such relationships for 30 plus years. Don't let this happen to you. Get out.

Red Flag No 34: They are pathological liars

Narcissists are shape-shifters, chameleons, Oscar winning actors, street angels, house devils. These skills go hand-in-hand with their inborn skill of pathological lying. They can't tell the truth without adding a few lies, because that would be too 'normal'. Lying spices things up nicely for them and though they generally have pretty good memories, they'll think nothing of saying they can't remember or completely denying things they've told you when they get to the 'Devaluing' stage. Which they invariably will. If you catch them out in the lies, they'll twist it to fit their version of the lie or they'll tell you you misheard or misunderstood them. They will make it look like you're stupid or dense because of it. As their lies and deceit grow bigger, you grow smaller inside.

Or if they've been caught on video or recorded, they'll swiftly switch to saying yes, they said it, but they were taken out of context, or that's actually not what they meant. They are also quite passionate in their self-defense, even to the point of being angry or outraged you would question them.

What's interesting (and dangerous) about this is that it's confusing and plays into the cognitive dissonance experience again. Normal people don't do this, and you're maybe still trying to figure this person out and not aware you're dealing with a full-blown narcissist. So perhaps you give them the benefit of the doubt. Or you start doubting yourself. You actually begin questioning your own version of events, even in the face of incontrovertible facts. That is scary.

They also lie by omission. They might say 'Oh I spent a few hours at a club with some work colleagues' when in fact they went to a strip club *after* having a drink with work colleagues. You're only ever getting half of the story.

They embellish the truth to beef up their egos and impress you or to outdo you if you've achieved something at work. If they got a pat on the back at work or a small bonus, they'll convince you that they're about to be appointed CEO.

They delude themselves, because they have NPD. They choose to believe everyone adores them, thinks they are special, brilliant, gorgeous or that the world owes them everything, simply because that's what they believe about themselves. Truth has nothing to do with it because they believe so many of their own lies. As one meme that showed up on my FB Feed recently said:

'No one gets more upset than a narcissist being accused of something they definitely did'!

Exactly!

They also profoundly believe that their opinion is the only one. They are always right. They have a monopoly on truth, their opinion is all that matters, and nothing you say or think is of any importance.

How to avoid the trap – my advice

My mother (God rest her!), once said to me 'You can protect yourself from a thief. You can lock your things up. But you can't protect yourself from a liar. People who lie are far more dangerous.' And she was right. If you suspect the person you are with is a narcissist (and by this point in the book, you should be in no doubt), know one thing for sure: you cannot believe a single word that comes out of their mouths.

You can protect yourself by keeping a journal or notebook about what's going on. This will help you to validate your own reality when they try to Gaslight you. Don't waste your time showing them your evidence, because as I've said, they'll just twist it out of shape. Just keep this for your own sanity whilst you are evaluating the whole relationship and I hope, making plans to leave them.

Red Flag No 35: Sex becomes a nightmare

Sex is one of the most important elements of a relationship because it's the one thing that differentiates it from all other relationships. You also open yourself up in a much more vulnerable way with an intimate partner so when it comes to sex with a narcissist, it soon becomes a huge turn-off. In the beginning, it's amazing, mind-blowing or at the very least, good enough. But as with everything in Narcland, sex is just another tool to manipulate, control, exploit and destroy you.

There are lots of different scenarios that might play out when it comes to sex, so let's a have a look at some of the ins and outs (excuse the pun) of sex with a narcissist.

They are generous in bed but...

Somatic narcissists are generally expert lovers and will treat you to multiple orgasms, sensual foreplay and oral sex. You'll be in sexual heaven for a time – usually the love bombing time, but what you don't know is this amazing sex is not about you, it's all about the narcissist 's ego. They pride themselves on being sexual athletes and on the positive fuel they'll get when you tell them they're the best lover you've ever had.

Screenplay/scripted sex

Some narcissists have a screenplay in their head about how they want sex to be. This could come from watching porn or some other idealized/romanticized fantasy they want to re-enact with you. They will tell you exactly how to position yourself, what to say and will direct your performance throughout. They don't care about your enjoyment or satisfaction. When they get you into this initially, you'll go along because you'll think it's a sexy adventure, but it'll soon wear very thin and you'll hate the thought of having to do this again. If you complain, you'll be called selfish, a prude or some other negative comment that makes you feel inadequate.

Boring sex

If a vulnerable narcissist has targeted you for example, it may not have been great because they're typically asexual and often will rely on you to show them the sex ropes. You'll find this endearing and sweet! But before long, you'll realize that they are just bored with it and they don't want sex at all! Your efforts to get them interested will result in you being called oversexed or a nymphomaniac. They are just not interested but they want to make it look like it's your fault for wanting it in the first place. Remember how they love to blame? And of course, you'll feel rejected, unattractive, unlovable and you'll make do with no sex at all.

You have to fit their mold

The more experienced Somatic will usually be able to read your sexual vibe enough to match it and make you happy in the early stages, but the less accomplished narcissists may not, and they will try their usual techniques, not realizing that not everyone has the same sexual buttons. If you try to suggest they try this or that instead, they'll get offended and blame you because 'It's worked fine with everyone else I've ever been with'. They can't take criticism, they blame you for everything and this applies equally to sex when they can't satisfy you, so if you fail to climax, it's your fault because you are probably frigid. They may also then use your 'criticism' of them as an excuse to withhold or refuse sex with you again. And of course, they'll blame you because you've said they're no good (even though that's not what you've said at all), so why bother? It gives them perfect excuse not to.

Sex is abusive / violent

Unfortunately, the sex becomes violent and abusive for a lot of women and you'll be forced to comply whether you like it or not. This may range from your partner grabbing your breasts/genitals or forcing you to go down on them, to rape. The subject of rape in marriage has long been controversial but if you are forcefully taken despite your protests, that is rape, whether you're married to the perpetrator or not. This is intolerable and you should not be prepared to put up with this under any circumstances.

Porn addiction

This is quite common in narcissists and it's no surprise because porn objectifies women and 99% of the time, sex is about female domination and male gratification. It's also, as you'll know if you've watched porn, devoid of any emotional connection. Whilst there is nothing wrong in using porn to spice up your sex life if that's your thing, obsessive watching (either furtively or blatantly) is a big sign of trouble. One woman reported her husband used to watch porn and then jump on top of her to 'finish himself off'.

The narcissist will often expect you to behave like porn actresses because having watched so much of it, they've come to believe that this is how women behave during sex. Studies have also shown that over-exposure to porn reduces a man's ability to sustain erection and also desensitizes them to real sex by raising the stimulation threshold bar so high it makes it more difficult, if not impossible, to sustain 'normal' sexual relations. They may also be taking Viagra but even that can fail to help them 'perform'.

Orgasmic pretending

The female narcissist will easily fool her besotted lover because she's better at faking it than Meg Ryan, in that very famous (and fabulous) scene in 'When Harry Met Sally'. Female narcissists are often addicted to any adrenaline rush they can find as a means of stimulation, so they'll want to 'dress up', talk dirty, role-play, involve you in risky outdoor sexual behavior or handcuff you top and bottom to the bedposts. Such theatrics can take over inside (and outside!) the bedroom and you never get any more 'normal' sex.

I've got a headache

Female narcissists, once they've got you under their spell, might stop giving you sex altogether because it's not giving them any fuel. They find their excitement in other ways, including depriving you of sex. They may start out saying they've got a headache, they're too tired, they're not in the mood and eventually they'll start calling you out for having 'sex on the brain' or call you a 'pervert'. Ridiculous, but it's done.

It's mechanical and soulless

If they do get down to it, it's often mechanical, robotic, without any real emotion, connection or tenderness and it leaves you feeling used, empty, lonely and longing for that powerful emotional connection you know should go together with the physical union.

They prefer masturbation

There's nothing wrong with masturbating but the narcissist's use of it, as you'll probably guess, is not going to be a pleasant experience for you. They will often play with themselves in front of you but reject you if you try to get involved. They'll tell you they'd rather do this than F*** you, or they will use you as an object while they get themselves off.

They'll force you into sexual activity that repulses you

They may be into S&M, threesomes, group sex, or some other sexual fetish you find highly offensive. However, their powers of persuasion are such that they can emotionally coerce or blackmail you into going along with these acts. You'll do it because you're so in love with them and afraid of losing them, but what you will be doing in the process is losing yourself. You will come away from each encounter feeling used, abused, guilty, ashamed and dirty. And the narcissist will use your participation in the future to further abuse you. They may threaten to expose you, call you depraved (remember they project their inner 'stuff' onto you) and you'll find yourself caught in a sexual trap you don't know how to escape.

Sex in public

Narcissists are exhibitionists and will often try to force you into having sex in risky or public places. They are excited by the real risk of being seen and have no shame about it, nor do they care it makes you uncomfortable. If you object, you'll be admonished for being boring, prudish and not adventurous enough for them. Once again, they're instilling the fear of losing them in you and you'll go against your instincts and comply.

They consider sex too primitive for them

The cerebral narcissist considers sex demeaning, degrading and disgusting. They consider their superior intellect puts them above wanting or needing such primitive, carnal desires. If you marry one and have agreed to have children, the only time you'll get sex is to get you pregnant.

They fire you up then cool you down

This is another trick they play. They'll send you erotic messages about what they want to do to you when they next see you and get you all hot and bothered at the thought of some exciting sex. When they show up, they'll switch off the sex vibe. This will cause you to wonder why, and you'll immediately think you're not looking your best or they 've gone off you, or they don't fancy you enough. None of this will be true. The truth is they have deliberately misled you with blatant sexual teasing and promises, which they fully intended not to deliver on. They will enjoy seeing your confusion and will use any advances you make to brush you off.

They want it, NOW!

Hypersexual narcissists will want sex frequently, and if you turn them down, they'll get angry or upset with you. They fail to realize you might be exhausted or just not in the mood. They don't care about your feelings because your job is to be there for them 24/7 and give them whatever they want, whenever they want it and that applies equally to sex. Often you'll just comply to get it over with, get them off your case or just so you can get your head down and get some sleep.

You love sex but...

The other side of this coin is if you're highly sexed yourself and you really enjoy sex, they will have discovered this about you as soon as you began your sexual relationship so they will deprive you of it now because they know it's going to make you suffer. You can't win in the sexual stakes with a narcissist. If you love it, they will deprive you. If you hate it, they will force it on you.

If you consider all those scenarios, what you'll see is typical narcissistic selfishness gets right down to the core of even the most intimate act between couples. You are never going to have a loving, fulfilling, satisfying sex life with a narcissist.

Some REAL examples of sex with narcissists

At this point, I want to share with you some harsh sex realities that have been shared with me and which illustrate most of the points I have covered in this section. I got more comments on this question of sex than any other I've asked in my groups. So, I'm sharing them to demonstrate to you the kind of reality you can expect to encounter if you enter into sexual congress with a narcissist.

I am extremely grateful to all these people for their honesty and I hope their stories will help you to see that sex within a narcissistic relationship is not where you want to be. These people all started out by being Love-Bombed, falling for the seduction of the Romantic Predator, and suffering because of it. Some of them are still stuck in these relationships and I hope and pray they can find their way out and find good, healthy loving sex instead of this nightmare they are living now.

So here they are...

'Thought he was a stud, but he was really a dud. But I had to stroke his ego.'

Mercy Shag...

'Mine was very highly sexed, wanted it morning, noon and night and would get very upset if I turned him down. It was normally because I was just exhausted taking care of our children alone; he did not participate in night feeds or early mornings with the children. If I wasn't in the mood but had what I called a 'mercy shag', he would be obsessed with making sure I orgasmed, as if he needed to show that he could make me enjoy sex even if I wasn't in the mood. I faked it more than once so I could get some much-needed rest. Even before kids when I had more time, energy and a higher libido, if I didn't orgasm he would see it as a personal slight, like I was not appreciative of his sexual prowess!!!'

Then I would be worthy of his penis...

*'Sex/intimacy and affection was withheld almost overnight after I said, "I do". I hopelessly waited 14 years due to the many excuses and sometimes blame as to why we didn't have sex. **Excuses were:** I*

am tired, stressed from work to finally admitting a few years later to me he had ED (Erectile Dysfunction). He couldn't use Viagra as a pilot (not true), they were too expensive, could not use them while on antibiotics (not true). **Blame was:** Maybe if I went to the gym, maybe if I made more money, maybe if I was doing more of his activity, maybe if I didn't wear pajamas in winter (easily removable). Then I would be worthy of his penis, right? He was not even willing to serve my needs in other ways. No holding hands and hugs either. Two months after I left, he had a new girlfriend and a Viagra prescription.'

Sex was not good enough sober...

'Sex was very awkward. The foreplay usually lasted hours and I would get tired and want to stop and he would talk nasty when I got to that point. He would talk about other people and call me dirty names. If I wanted sex, he would say no and give me some reason, but if I said no he would do it anyway. Apparently, sex was also not good enough sober and even the first night we spent together I had to put on a nighty that he degraded and had no interest in, until after he had convinced me to take a pill with him. Then everything was great, very weird.'

I shouldn't have shown him how to make love...

'He used the excuse that he wanted sex all the time and I shouldn't have shown him how to make love. It started out very mechanical in the beginning, quite soulless but I wasn't having any of that nonsense. If we do it we both get satisfied - which of course didn't happen - as when he was in an abusive stage he would just get himself off with no affection but in the end he kissed, touched, even oral. I guess if he wanted it so often, he had to develop extra "skills" lol but yes, he did use it as a power tool. He would talk at me brainwashing me during it, that I was the only one for him and marry me and I would never stray and because he was 11 years younger he'd say 'I'll always want to f*** you no matter how old you get (the old backhand degradation passive-aggressive style) He has never loved anyone as much as he loves me. We need to be a team and have each other's back, where are you going to get great sexual chemistry that we have anywhere else? No one will ever love you like I do. I'll look after you forever. You're the best f*** I've ever had. And the list went on. The guy sure knew how to get in my head with his constant talking himself up.'

I never, ever climaxed with him...

'It felt mechanical, like I was with a robot. There was no heart involved. He was very experienced, but the soul aspect was gone. I never ever climaxed with him and that should have been a huge red flag for me. There was no sensuality; it was as the saying goes, "Slam, bam, thank you mam!" I kept thinking it would get better, but it just got grosser, if that's even a word. Heartless is a perfect description.'

Automatic pilot...

'Automatic pilot. During sleep. 3/4/5 times a night. Nothing would prevent this, even peri-menopausal bleeding. He'd be all lovely and put the gory sheets in the washing machine. So much physical contact made me get used to it and welcome it. But there was no soul to it.'

Not a peck on the cheek in 14 years...

'It died the moment the ring was on my finger. Not so much as a peck on the cheek for the past 14 years in a 14-year marriage. He wasted no time in wrapping me in so much debt that I couldn't escape. I'm here to do all the work and he's here to enjoy himself at my expense.'

I was merely a pussy...

'If we ever did have sex, it was as though I was merely a pussy-- no touching, no kissing, no foreplay (although I gave him oral so many times- in a year and a half I received oral 3 times)... eyes always closed, no sounds, hands at side (only 3 times was he doing the 'work' and the last time he was on top he had gained so much weight I was almost suffocated)... it would be over in 10 minutes and no kissing, touching, cuddling, nothing.'

Used it as a means for control/punishment...

'Withheld it if it was me that initiated, but then gave me no choice if it was him wanting to start, and I wasn't wanting to. Completely love-bombed me with it when we first got together - multiple times per day, and then even proposed during sex after we had only been together for around 5 months. Then proceeded to tell anyone that would listen to him, about that, not caring that I felt uncomfortable with him doing that.'

I would lie there like a rag doll and pray for it to be over...

'My Narc is 66 years old and all he thought of most of the time was sex - it drove me crazy! He would lie and play with himself and look like a retard. It was the most irate moments for me. I too never ever felt any pleasure or satisfaction having sex with him. I would just lie there like a rag doll and pray for it to be over. He would want sex 3 to 4 days a week. For me sex with him was a big mission because I was just allowing it to get him to stop playing with himself in front of me. So yes, sex with a Narc is like sex with a blowup doll no emotions at all. I simply hated it!'

It's always about him...

'It's always all about him. He has to have it more often, he has to be told he's the best, he wants me to tell him about the other guys I was with during it, he thinks he's the ultimate at oral and rarely has any idea what romance and foreplay is. More times than not I end up faking orgasms and the funny part is he doesn't even know the difference.'

Told me the day after we married that he was not attracted to me...

'Mine told me the day after marriage that he was not attracted to me. Told me he was animalistically attracted to his last wife, but what we have is better, that we are "spiritually attracted".

I felt like a whore...

'After a while I even felt like a whore. I would always look for money on my side table even though there never was. But that was the feeling I had.'

Oral sex is evil, but he likes to receive it...

'It's about him. He comes and gets oral. I didn't come and never had oral. He is a religious Narc and thinks that giving oral sex is evil, but he likes to receive it.'

Boasted he'd slept with over 80 women...

'Goodness where shall I begin? Boasts about previous sexual conquests. Mine told me quite proudly that he'd slept with over 80 women. He then continued to boast about prostitutes and massage parlors he'd visited - while I was still with him.'

It's so sad when you have to pleasure yourself...

'In the very beginning (first month) it was frequent, he would look at me, kiss me, go down on me.. then it went to once a week, then once a month. I had talked with him in the beginning (wrong move) about how I've been in relationships where the sex essentially vanishes, and that tells me something is wrong... well, he became that relationship also... *sex nearly vanished. He went to the doctor about 7 months in and was told he couldn't take Viagra because he had high blood pressure (which of course he hadn't done anything about)... So my needs, as usual, get pushed to the side... it's incredibly sad when you have to pleasure yourself while your fiancé is in the other room because it has been so long... he really made me feel unattractive, undesirable and unwanted...and I almost signed up for a lifetime of that!'*

I ask too much, I'm too fat, I'm too skinny...

'My Ex used sex as a punishment. He would constantly deny it. I've never been with a man who wanted it so little. I got blamed constantly for him not wanting it. He would say anything from I ask to much, I'm too fat, I'm too skinny, I'm a prude etc.'

He only really gets off if he knows he's hurting me...

'My husband is 55. He doesn't get completely hard but can go for quite a while. He is on the sex offenders' register for raping a woman twenty years younger than him fourteen years ago. He bends me into uncomfortable positions, forces anal even when I have screamed, tries to "deep throat" me which I can't do, forces a vibrator up at the same time as his dick, never kisses me or goes down on me...

Despite all this I have enjoyed a lot of the sex as he knows I like it rough but he always goes that bit too far, he only really gets off if he knows he is hurting me or forcing me, and he rarely comes which he attributes to taking Paxil. After he choked me on the floor one night, he followed me into the spare bedroom, pulled my shorts off and started having sex with me while I cried. I have no doubt that the act of choking me turned him on as he has put his hand and once his belt around my neck during sex previously and loves to restrict my breathing by sitting on me and using his 6 foot 4, 100lbs more than me weight to dominate me.'

(**Note:** I am relieved to report that this woman is no longer with her monster husband and is now living safely, thousands of miles away from him on a different continent).

Where do I start?

'Oh, where do I start? Sexual addictions, porn, sexting, hook ups, one night stands, hiring escorts/prostitutes, constantly flirting and charming women, constantly needing continuous and multiple women for emotional and sexual affairs while he was with me, sending nude videos and pictures to women and vice versus, X-rated and regular dating sites, cheating... all of this has bothered me and affected me more than even his alcoholism, smoking, control, meanness, degrading, discarding, abuse, put downs, disrespecting, etc. Yes, all affected me and I did not deserve any of this, but the part I cannot get over at all is all the other continuous women/sex - because he was distant, emotionless, and not affectionate, flirty, charming, horny, or sexual with me at all, or very minimally. I'm a sensual, beautiful woman who would enjoy sex every day, why was I not enough for him?'

There was always an issue with sex toys...

'There was always an issue with sex toys. I'm pretty wild and like to keep things interesting as she enjoyed it as well. I'd put them away and then when she'd come over, she'd start badgering me and saying I'd left them at my other bitch's house, which was total nonsense. It was a week-long torture session no matter what I did, no matter what I said. She would not give up, even when I showed her where I'd stored the toys.'

I'm extremely lonely, depressed and heartbroken...

'We have been married 10 years and 2 months. For the last 6 years he wanted sex almost every day. The last 4 years I'm lucky if I have sex once a month. He used to absolutely love satisfying me orally but that hasn't happened in over a year. ONLY THING HE WANTS IS ME TO GET HIM OFF AND I GET Nothing. I'M EXTREMELY LONELY, DEPRESSED AND HEARTBROKEN.'

No emotional connection at all during intimacy...

'My first Narc Ex-wife pretended to be a virgin when we got married and she was 9 years older than me. She was lousy in bed and used sex as manipulation. The second Ex was BPD*, and she could not get enough sex, wanted fetish sex and then abruptly stopped the sex because her bipolar meds made her less desiring for sex. How stupid of me. She was having sex behind my back, we divorced 14 months later. The last Narc (3 months ago), I was very awake to her ploys of sending naked pics, using sex to hasten a relationship and she then subtly hinted that couples when their relationship starts, the sex is frequent, but it tapers down after a while. I cut this relationship after 2 months. But 2 months was enough to do a bit of damage too. She was lousy in bed, non-existent foreplay, but expected me to satisfy her. My experience is the sex was used to hook me with all the narcs and in the end, they were all lousy in bed. No emotional connection at all during the intimacy.'

*Borderline Personality Disorder

And I want to share one more as it clearly demonstrates the 'push/pull', guilt-tripping and subsequent confusion narcissistic sexual manipulation causes...

He exhausted and confused and hurt me...

'Mine would cause huge rows with me if ever I 'dared' agree to go to a friend's birthday, or a 'girls night' with friends.... to the point he would ridicule me and make me feel dreadful until I would sometimes then end up crying whilst trying to do my makeup - and *then I would either say "okay I won't go" or would go silent on him. He'd then come right over in my personal space and say he was sorry, that of course he didn't mind me going out really... that of course he wanted me to have a good time and see my friends really... he would then immediately try and initiate sex. With my eyes still wet from crying.*

*When I would be confused and holding myself back in that bizarre moment, he would then say things like "You're making me feel disgusting, but I can't help myself, I'm so sorry, I just need to make love to you, you look beautiful.." and he would say "is it weird that you're making me want to f*** you right now?" I was upset, with my head down, not even wanting to look at him after all he'd just been saying to me whilst I tried to get ready.*

I was always just so 'numb' by then, that I really didn't want to be near him - but often would just go through the motions so to speak when he would do that to me, and so he would then say to me "what the hell are you acting like a rag doll for? See what I mean, you don't even find me attractive do you... well I hope you find someone better out there tonight!!" I would grit my teeth and think "maybe this might calm him down" as he did what he wanted with me.

I barely had the energy to even respond to him. He exhausted and confused and hurt me. And made me feel I was always doing something wrong, when I never was. I had never heard of emotional abuse back then. I just used to think he was a bit insecure. Ugh.'

These real-life examples make for sad reading, don't they? What should be loving, exciting and something to look forward in a relationship has become a battleground for most people involved with narcissists. You don't even get kisses and cuddles unless the narcissist is bouncing back to the love bombing stage and they only do that to keep you tied and bonded to them so they keep getting their fuel, and they can continue abusing you. Your needs are never met, they simply don't care.

How to avoid the trap – my advice

Do I really need to add anything here? Ask yourself what do you think my advice is right now? I'm pretty sure you can guess. But for the record, KNOW no matter how good sex is in the beginning, during that all important 'Love Bombing' stage, it's not going to last and you're going to end up in a similar situation (or worse) as the people who have shared their stories with me. If the sex is lousy to begin with, do you honestly think it will get better? No, it won't. Remember what I said back in the early part of the book, about not having sex on the first dates? Get to know the person first and be as certain as you can that you're not getting into bed with a narcissist.

Red Flag No 36: They ruin every social occasion for you

Narcissists, as we now know, crave attention and they have to be at the center of the Universe, always. If there is anything going on that puts the focus on other people, they will do everything in their power to ruin the occasion for you.

For example, let's say you have a birthday party to attend together. They will start bitching as you are getting ready. You don't look good. They will criticize your clothes, hair, make-up, jewelry. They'll say they don't want to go. If you suggest you'll go alone, you'll get a tirade of abuse and accusations. They will make you late. When you eventually get there, they will behave badly, making derogatory comments about you in front of people, talking down to others and making every moment of the occasion a misery for you.

If they are too fond of their egos to display their true character in public, you'll get the passive-aggressive approach or quiet, underhanded comments whispered at you so no one else can hear. Passive-aggression is an insidious form of abuse. It can be framed as what sounds like compliments to others, but underneath, there are subtle put-downs. It's covert abuse in its finest form. An example in this situation could be, your partner says to the host of the event 'Oh Lauren wasn't really feeling up to tonight, but I convinced her she couldn't miss such an important occasion!' This is not only an outright lie; it makes you look bad in front of the host, who might wonder why you didn't want to attend their party. If you ask them later why they said it, they'll twist it, say you've imagined it or that's not what they said at all. What is *wrong* with you?

On the way home, they will spend the entire time criticizing everyone and everything about the event, complaining about what a waste of time it was and how could you be so selfish as to drag them along to it when you know they didn't want to go. You'll eventually be numb from listening to them and you'll fall into bed in an exhausted, depressed heap – if they let you.

On the other hand, if there is an event they want to go to, you're expected to do cartwheels of joy for them. They'll expect you to drop everything to go with them, whenever and wherever they want. They will also deliberately double book on a special occasion of yours and expect you to cancel your plans to go with them. You'll be expected to be dressed to perfection and on your best behavior. Even if you've told them months in advance about your special occasion, they'll deny you ever did. You and your needs don't matter and you have to get this harsh truth into your head.

How to avoid the trap – my advice

If you're stuck in this relationship and can't get out, you have to learn how to NOT let them get to you. Easier said than done, but it can be done. You could try not telling them about any given event and just going alone. Deal with the consequences when you get back - at least, you will have had a good night without their constant barrage of criticism. But, see my caveat about violence a bit further below.

Or you could try the Grey Rock technique, which is basically non-reaction. You let everything they say roll off you like water off a duck's back. You let them rant and rave, but you take no notice of it. If you argue back or try to defend your position, you just give them more ammunition and more fuel. Grey Rocking takes that away from them. It's a skill if you can learn to apply it, will serve you well until you can get out. So, let me explain a bit more about how to work the Grey Rock technique and once again, I've borrowed this from a blog I wrote but I really think it will be helpful to include it here for you.

Understanding the term Grey Rock and what it means is particularly useful if you're in a narcissistic relationship and you simply can't get out. Typically the reasons you can't get out have to do with finances or children or when you're planning your escape strategy but you know it's going to take time or you're at the stage where you're thinking of finding that way out and knowing what Grey Rocking is and how to use it, can give you some very much-needed respite from the constant knife-edge life you're living with a narcissist.

The term Grey Rock was apparently coined by a blogger named Skylar, in a blog entitled 'The Gray Rock Method of Dealing with Psychopaths'. I've also heard from another source the concept was devised by the British Special Forces to protect soldiers captured during the war. Whatever the origins, the 'method' is about being as boring, uninteresting, un-reactive and neutral as a grey rock - unless you're a Geologist, grey rocks are just boring, aren't they?

One of the many things narcissists have in spades is tenacity... the tenacity to keep on picking on you, belittling you, baiting you, trying every trick in their inexhaustive handbook of narcissistic tricks to get a rise out of you... it's mentally exhausting and when you constantly keep trying to defend yourself, argue, reason, placate and otherwise mollify them, you're draining your own energy, giving yourself no mental peace or space to breathe.

Applying the 'Grey Rock' technique can free you from all this and once you get your head around that, you're going to be able to get some peace. Because once the Narc realizes they can't get that all-important fuel from you, they'll stop. They'll stop long enough to give you space to think and have that bit of peace your brain is craving.

This is not to say they won't come back at you with renewed enthusiasm, after they've given you the silent treatment, stomped around, sulked or done whatever they needed to… they will come back, guaranteed. Then you continue Grey Rocking. Remember narcissists and psychopaths crave stimulation and if you stop giving them any, you really take the wind out of their sails.

Narcissists are good at reading their victims, but they need to get inside your head to know which buttons to push. That's how they, in Romantic Predator mode, seduced you in the first place and how they've mastered the art of their vile abuse. If you stop reacting, arguing, crying, trying to reason with them and give them nothing, they'll be flummoxed. They might seem like mind readers a lot of the time, but the fact is they're not mind readers, they are just reading what you're giving them. And every time you try to do what normal people do to iron out the kinks in the relationship (which by the way, is an out-and-out impossibility with a narcissist), you're giving them the information they need to hurt you more.

What exactly is Grey Rocking when you get down to it? Quite simply, as I've mentioned, it's being as boring and non-reactive as you possibly can. Think bland… the blandest of the bland! Think of the most boring non-conversation you could ever possibly have and give only that to the narcissist.

Here are four tips on how to Grey Rock like a pro!

Tip No 1

You must decide to clam up and keep all your real thoughts and feelings to yourself. The less the Narc knows about what's really going on in your head, the better. Even if you are in a rage or a puddle of angst over something they've said or done, DON'T show it. Think 'Poker Face!' and don't let your emotions show.

Tip No 2

Don't start conversations with them AT ALL, and don't ask questions. Think of Grey Rocking as the 'real life' equivalent of No Contact – or Low Contact. You're aiming to keep communication and therefore opportunities to give them 'fuel, and yourself stress, to an absolute minimum.

Tip No 3

If they ask you questions, make your answers as brief and bland as possible. Don't go into any but the most basic details. Yes and No will suffice when possible. If they probe, be as creatively dull as you possibly can be.

Here's an example... just to give you the idea of how to be creatively dull...

If your Partner (P) asks:

P: How was work today?
You: Same as always
P: Were you busy?
You: Yes/No (opt for No even if you were, because yes might invite more questions)
P: Who did you have lunch with?
You: No one (even if you did, lie about that and say no one)

P: What did you have for lunch?
You: Sandwich.
P: What kind of sandwich?
You: Bread and cheese

Ok, so you get the idea. It takes a bit of practice and internal restraint to get into the swing of this, because we're programmed to be social beings and to respond when spoken to or answer questions, so we automatically start filling in the blanks and offering up information without thinking about it.

If you're embroiled in a relationship with a narcissist, you have to learn a whole new set of coping skills. Bear in mind when you start doing this, they are very probably going to start telling you you're boring, idiotic, a useless conversationalist and say infantile things like:

'What, cat got your tongue?'

and other childish barbs. Your job is to nod and say 'Yeah'… with a boring sigh, like you don't have the energy for anything more. They'll probably say a lot worse if those barbs don't get a reaction from you. Don't take the bait and start trying to defend yourself. KEEP GREY ROCKING! Say things like 'Yeah'… 'Ok'. You can also just murmur 'Mmmm' a lot of the time! If they keep pressing you for a response, which they very well might, say something like 'You're right. You're always right.' That will please them because it feeds into their ridiculous egos. Just don't say it sarcastically. Say it with a resigned air to it. But, in the back of your mind, you know this is an act that YOU are putting on for them.

You can practice this by thinking of all the kinds of questions your partner usually asks you or the kinds of comments he or she makes and start making up responses and saying them in your head. Boring, boring, boring responses! Then start gradually using them.

Tip No 4

You can also buy yourself time when the narcissist is asking questions requiring an answer, and say things like 'maybe', 'we'll see', or 'possibly', in cases where you're being asked to commit to something you're not sure about. Get used to using these strategies to buy yourself some thinking time and space. Never tell them this is something you are doing intentionally. That will completely blow your cover and render your attempts useless, but be prepared for them to notice this change in your behavior. You might find them staring at you or hovering around you, trying to intimidate you, but keep your cool. Don't react, don't respond.

Warning... having said all that...

When you first do this, they might well react with anger and start shouting, threatening and trying to scare you. But – and I say this with a big caveat – only do this Grey Rocking if you know your partner is NOT physically violent. Don't let this be an excuse that provokes their anger and causes them to start hitting you or destroying things... if that's the case and they are prone to violence, for the love of God file a police report and get a restraining order.

I just wanted to make that clear because I don't want you to do anything which might put you in physical danger – so I'm talking about Grey Rocking as a tactic that will work if you've got a non-violent narcissist to deal with. So, assuming you do, let's go back to what to expect... anger, very likely, but you have to remain cool. Let them rant and rave. They are only trying to extract a reaction from you. If they don't get it, their anger will soon die down.

Expect, as I mentioned, possibly the silent treatment (Red Flag No 37, coming up), derision, sarcastic comments, cajoling, laughter... just run through all your partner's typical tactics and be prepared for all of them to come to the party. But remain calm, bland and boring in the face of all of them. If you can perfect this 'Narc neutralizing technique', you'll find they will back off and leave you alone, because it's taking far too much effort for zero gain – i.e., fuel, from you and they will look elsewhere for that fuel.

Before I bring this to a close, there's a couple of things I want to mention here: whilst Grey Rock is a very handy tool to have in your arsenal against a narcissist, remember that you don't want to shut yourself off in this way from everyone else. It's important that you make that clear distinction in your head. You only want to numb yourself to the narcissist, not to other people who are important in your life – if you still have any left and haven't been totally isolated from them! Grey Rock will not cause dissociation, as has sometimes been said. You are very in touch with yourself when you Grey Rock. You just CHOOSE not to engage in a meaningful way. Think of it as being deliberately closed and keeping your cards close to your chest.

And reach out to a trusted friend or your support group, so you can share your thoughts and feelings with them about what you are going through. Don't bottle it all up and try to go it alone because isolation like this on top of the constant narcissistic abuse, is seriously detrimental to your emotional health.

Now these tips are not going to heal you completely and make your life perfect, but they will give you some peace and breathing space while you figure out what to do next. I've had many women in my group try these tips out and they've messaged me that it definitely works. Grey Rock is not a long-term solution to healing from narcissistic abuse. For that to happen, you'll very likely need to work with a therapist and of course, I said I'd keep repeating it – you need to get out of the relationship. No matter how long it might take.

Red Flag No 37: The Silent Treatment/ Stonewalling/Ghosting

These tactics hurt just as much as the verbal abuse you'll be regularly subjected to. The Silent Treatment is just that – the narcissist refuses to engage with you and you might as well be invisible. This is an extremely hurtful kind of treatment because it makes you feel so totally invalidated and worthless. Your pleas to be heard, to apologize, to explain, to rationalize, to make up, all fall on deaf ears that deliberately do not want to hear anything you have to say. Ignoring you like this is just another form of punishment. When this happens, you'll feel isolated, lonely and depressed.

What is also important to note is silent treatment like this has negative effects on your brain. Studies have shown that the anterior cingulate cortex in your brain is responsible for detecting different levels of pain and the silent treatment activates this zone. Not only that, it also affects your autoimmune system because of the stress it causes. I'm going to go into health a bit more shortly, but just wanted to note this here. The Silent Treatment is damaging to you emotionally and physically.

Stonewalling

This is when your partner withdraws from a conversation or discussion and refuses to consider your concerns. They may ignore you, change the subject, and give vague or dismissive responses or derogatory, invalidating responses that simply do nothing to address the subject you're trying to discuss with them. This tactic also invalidates and isolates you, but it makes you more desperate for attention, effectively putting the narcissist in more control over your emotions.

Stonewalling also often devolves into gaslighting or other forms of devaluing to emotionally unseat you and get you to keep giving them fuel. They want to see you suffer and hear you beg. The Silent Treatment will usually follow because the narcissist wants to prove his or her power by denying you any access at all to conversation.

This is of course denying you basic rights and respect as a human being. Who the hell treats people like this? Narcissists do, because they want to belittle, demean and make you feel insignificant and invisible.

How to avoid the trap – my advice

The most important thing you need to know here is it's NOT you at fault. You have done nothing wrong but behave in a normal fashion, and you do NOT deserve this abhorrent treatment. If you're being subjected to these tactics, reframe the context of what is going on here. Consider this a time of peace to think for yourself. Take this silent or alone time to really reflect on this relationship and ask yourself: is this how you want to continue your life?

Grab a pen and a journal and start with two simple columns - Pros and Cons – of being in this relationship. This is an excellent way of seeing what's really going on, without the 'rose tinted' spectacles. Be really honest here and see how quickly the 'Cons' column fills up. Keep this journal hidden and safe and go back to it every chance you get, and add more to those columns. When you're in an abusive relationship like this, you tend to overlook or conveniently 'forget' the abusive times, particularly when your partner bounces back with love bomb crumbs to keep you hooked. This is known as Intermittent Reinforcement and it's a well-known psychological tactic to keep you bonded. Having everything written down in black and white can help you see the reality you are living and give you the courage to start planning your exit strategy.

Ghosting

This takes the Silent Treatment and Stonewalling to a whole different level. The narcissist simply vanishes out of your life, with no explanation. This can happen at any stage of the relationship and leave you reeling with unanswered questions. The depth and level of confusion you'll feel will depend on how much time you've spent getting to know this person or how deep you are in the relationship. It could be you've been chatting on a dating site for weeks or even months and everything seemed to be going great; but suddenly they disappear. Poof! Gone. Or you were friends on Facebook, but one day you log in and go to messenger and they're nowhere to be found. You search their name, and nothing comes up. They have blocked (ghosted) you for no reason you can fathom. And you'll never find out, unless one day they decide to engage again and if they do, they will have some elaborate sob story to make you believe they had no choice and a whole lot of other BS you'd be very wise not to believe.

When you're in the relationship with them, even married to them, they may vanish for days, weeks, or for good. Remember I mentioned earlier on that they may have their own home you never get to see? This is often the reason why – so they have a bolthole to run to if they feel like it or need to. They keep these homes to escape to. Why they do this depends... if you are their 'Primary' source of fuel and they live with you most of the time, they may be using their bolthole to entertain/seduce 'Secondary' sources of fuel. These will often be one-night stands or short flings they engage in.

They also do it to punish, worry and stress you out even more. This ghosting extends to other forms of contact. You won't be able to reach them by phone, (bear in mind narcissists often have more than one phone) they won't respond to text messages. You'll be pacing up and down worrying yourself sick and your anxiety will be off the charts. Meanwhile they will be at home with their new supply or they'll be out looking for it. Wherever they are they won't be worrying about how you are feeling.

They may disappear because they have found a more exciting new supply of fuel. They may leave for good and you'll find yourself discarded.

If or when they do return, (this could be weeks, months or even years after the disappearing act) they'll behave as if nothing out of the ordinary has happened and why are you making such a fuss? Again, they will twist this around and make you feel guilty and stupid for acting up about it. If it's a recent return, you'll be so relieved you'll let it drop. You'll do this every time it happens. Over time you won't even notice how much of yourself and your basic human rights you have given up to this person. You will have managed down your expectations to the point that you are willing to accept whatever pathetic excuse they come up with. Their annihilation of your personality continues and you continue to allow it because you don't understand this level of manipulation, you don't understand that you are being systematically brainwashed and traumatized.

If they turn up after years, they will have some outrageous explanation as to why, as in one example I heard about: 'You told me to leave and not come back until I was ready to commit. Well here I am.' This was from a guy who discarded a woman and turned up out of the blue 7 years later. Another showed up 20 years later, with EXACTLY the same love bombing lines, songs, the lot, with the excuse that the break-up was 'Just a misunderstanding.' Despite the absurdity of these excuses, both these women took the guys back.

Keep in mind, even if you block them and have maintained No Contact for years, they may still find a way back in. Don't let this catch you unawares if it happens. If they do show up again, block them. Keep your defenses up and remember that unless you have done the deep healing work, you could still be vulnerable.

How to avoid the trap – my advice

I'd suggest the same process as for the Silent/Stonewalling treatment. Get your journal out and add this latest metaphorical punch in the gut to the diabolical treatment you've already allowed yourself to put up with, and really SEE what's going on in your relationship.

Wake up to the fact that this is NOT how people should be treating you. Realize you are better than this, you deserve respect and happiness and get to work on your exit strategy. When the narcissist comes swanning back in and acts as if nothing has happened, decide to act the same way. Do not ask where they've been, do not say you were worried, upset or missed them. This will confuse them because they'll be expecting a big show from you. Don't give them the satisfaction of providing that fuel to them. Remember Grey Rock? Use it here.

And focus on your exit plan but do this in secret. Do not give them any idea you are planning to leave, because if they feel threatened, that you're beginning to see through them, they will redouble their efforts with love bombing or, they will start putting their Smear Campaign plans in place, ready for when either they discard you or you them. Don't give them a head start.

Red Flag No 38: Triangulation

Triangulation is a tactic narcissists use to employ a third party by bringing them into the relationship (superficially or otherwise) in their attempts to belittle, confuse or worry you, create jealousy, fear of loss and causing you to vie for their attention and affections. Triangulation involves three people – the narcissist, their victim and the 'third party' who gets drawn into the drama, usually in a covert operation orchestrated by the narcissist. I should point out they can (and usually do) have several of these triangles operating at any one time. However, not all triangles are the same – there are two sides to triangulation – positive and negative.

Positive Triangulation

Positive triangulation is the tactic narcissists use to gain favor with other people - it could be your family, your friends, their family and friends, work colleagues, ex-partners, future potential partners and even complete strangers. Basically, just about anyone in your life, and in their life, will be a target for them to build a web of lies and deceit about you so they can gain more narcissistic supply or fuel from all concerned.

They use this positive triangulation to make themselves seem like angels, paint you as unstable, crazy, difficult, demanding and a thousand other things that are simply not true about you. This helps them gain sympathy – aka fuel – from the triangulation target, and it goes a long way to explaining why their subsequent Smear Campaigns against you can be so successful. They are so charming, convincing and believable, that can completely discredit you, even to people who you believed would never fall for such lies. Yes, even family and 'best friends' have been duped. They also have flying monkeys who serve as ambassadors to back them up whenever they need it.

Positive triangulation like this is also used to make you feel inadequate, inferior and worthless. For example, when your Narc openly flirts with another right in front of you or when a parent openly praises your sibling but never praises you. Very few people, when they are receiving praise, will EVER consider it's at someone else's cost… 99% of the time, they will just enjoy the compliment. In the case of flirting, if the flirting Narc is attractive, there's also a hidden agenda and they're probably looking at their next tasty narcissistic snack.

And of course, you realize this new person could be a threat to your relationship, so it sparks the fear in you that you could lose your partner. Obviously, this takes place when you are still in love and though confused and distressed most of the time in the relationship, you're still not ready to let go. You're afraid to lose this partner because you're still hanging on and hoping for a return to the golden days.

But the narcissist is doing this deliberately, to instill this fear of loss into you... to make you feel you're at risk of losing them to this new, attractive person they are flirting with. This causes you to want to please them even more, so you become more subservient, pliable and fall deeper under their spell and ultimately, their control.

Negative Triangulation

Negative triangulation is when there is an important person in your life who the narcissist sees as a threat – for example, your child or children. The Narc can't bear to see you giving your time and attention to anyone else, so they will do everything they can to disrupt, corrupt and destroy that relationship. They will try every trick in the book to drive a wedge between you and your child or whoever the person is who's important to you.

And it doesn't matter if you're caring for a sick, elderly parent... the narcissist hates illness and weakness of any kind and they have absolutely no compassion towards the sick... so if you're in this kind of situation, the Narc's hatred of you for caring for a sick person will intensify.

The people who can be used for triangulation by the narcissist include a selection of people who they have groomed (conned) into believing they are Mr. or Ms. Wonderful. Such people belong in the narcissist's 'harem', 'coterie' or the 'narcissist's army'. They are all your enemies.

How to avoid the trap – my advice

The harsh reality is you have to open your eyes and see what the narcissist is doing to you. If they regularly flirt in front of you, that's a huge red flag. Someone who loves and respects you just doesn't behave like that. Someone who loves you wants you to be happy, and wants you to feel safe. If you're in any doubt about their behavior, ask yourself: 'Would I do that to him/her?' Remember to tune into your emotional barometer. If their behavior is making you feel bad in any way, you need to listen and ask yourself why you are allowing this disrespect?

Research triangulation and start looking for the correlating behaviors in your relationship. Look for evidence. Once you find it, you'll realize this kind of behavior is not going to stop. Narcissists are incapable of changing and everything they do is geared to getting supply and destroying you in the process.

At the risk of sounding like a broken record: Your only answer is to get out. I know that's not going to be easy, but it is the only answer. No matter how long you've been in the relationship, no matter how scared you might be, you have to plan your exit strategy because if you don't you will spend the rest of your life in misery.

However, while you're planning your exit strategy, what you CAN do during this stage is to IGNORE the flirting. Don't let them see it's upsetting you. Put on your poker face! Grey Rock! By doing this, you deprive them of fuel and if you can perfect your poker face, they may at least let up on this particular tactic.

Red Flag No 39: They cheat on you

He said: 'Two things you don't do... cheat or talk bad about your partner.' Clearly he's been doing both. ' **(Comment in a Facebook Support Group)**

Narcissists are serial cheaters because they need to have a constant supply of fuel, and one source is never enough. They have their Primary and Secondary sources, so if they are living with you, then you are their Primary source. They will cheat sometimes surreptitiously and they'll deny any allegations or proof you come up with, whilst frequently accusing you of cheating, or they'll flaunt it in your face and tell you to accept it or leave.

I've heard this happen as in the example of another woman I talked to who told me her husband of over 30 years walked in one day and said he was in love with another woman and he was going to keep seeing her and she (his wife) would just have to accept it because she didn't have a choice. She put up with this just long enough for their children to get through their exams and then told him to go. I've also known many women who swore their husbands never cheated, but after the discard they started putting pieces of the jigsaw together and realized their partner had been cheating for years. Many women have to stay and put up with this for years before finally getting their heads on straight and deciding enough is enough and getting out.

Often when you are in a long-term relationship with a narcissist, you can't see the forest for the trees because the way they treat you is just so weird all the time anyway; they twist and turn everything into something else, so it's very easy for you to lose the threads of reality. You may also be confused because your emotional compass is 'off' due to the tactics they have been using.

If you are a 'secondary' source of supply, you'll only be seeing the narcissist at certain times. Do you have any idea what they are up to when not with you? The chances are high they are living with or married to someone else. That someone else would be their 'Primary' source of fuel.

Another thing they do is constantly ogle, admire or comment on attractive people. This could be in real life, people on TV and even if they don't say it, you get the feeling you don't match up. You're not as slim, attractive, successful or whatever and this is another nail in the coffin of your self-worth and confidence.

How to avoid the trap – my advice.

If you suspect someone is cheating on you, you are probably right. And if someone cheats on you once, they will do it again. Don't fall for the lies and promises it will never happen again. It will. If you don't want to be cheated on for the rest of your life, get out.

Red Flag No 40: They isolate you from family and friends

This is one of the most destructive things narcissists do. If they identify anyone in your circle who might see through them, they will immediately want to remove that threat. But they don't do this blatantly. They are cunning in how they tackle this one. They will initially act like they really like this person, and tell you they're happy you have such a great sister, or friend or whatever.

But then slowly, they'll pick up on something about that person and start criticizing them – but this will be done in a very subtle way. They'll make a comment like 'Your sister/friend is great but I sometimes think she's maybe a bit jealous of you.' This type of comment is designed to get you second-guessing yourself and thinking differently about this person. Or, they will lie outright about something your friend or sister said about you, but beg you not to mention it. They will say they are only telling you because they thought you really ought to know. And soon they will persuade you this person is no good for you and thus, drive a wedge between you. They will usually do this in the early stages of the relationship, when you are totally besotted with them and their powers of influence over you are so strong. They'll say things like:

- *I want us to spend all our spare time together*
- *Oh don't go out tonight... stay here with me instead*
- *I can't bear to spend a day/night without you*
- *Oh, you know I don't see eye-to-eye with 'so-and-so'... do we HAVE to go?*

- *Can we give it a miss this time?*

Whilst the initial isolation begins with subtlety, over time, it becomes more demanding or grounds for major battles, Silent Treatment, etc., so you'll find yourself giving in just to keep the peace.

They may take it as far as getting you to relocate, leaving everyone you know and love behind. They are frequent job hoppers, so it's easy enough for them to find a job in a different location and persuade you to move with them.

But isolating you from people is not enough. If you have hobbies, like to go to the gym, or have any kind of extra-curricular activities, they'll find a way to scupper those too. They'll accuse you of flirting with people at the gym. They'll buy a treadmill for the home so you can work out on that. They'll say your hobbies are a waste of time and money. They will even ruin your career, get you to stop studying for better qualifications, quit your job so that you don't have to travel or commute so much, or because you want to start a family, stop dressing the way you like and change your hairstyle.

In time, as their control over you gets stronger (and it will) they will outright forbid you to do anything they don't want you to do. Which is everything. Gradually they will isolate you from all your family, friends and everything you enjoyed doing. One day you'll wake up and realize you're alone and have no one but them anymore.

They may also take it to the level of taking away or monitoring your phone and Laptop. They may also insist on having all your passwords so they can access your bank account, Social Media and anything else they like. Ultimately, you've got no say and no life of your own. You're living like a prisoner and your partner is the jailor.

There are several reasons why narcissists isolate you in this way. Top of the list is to manipulate and control you, thereby securing plenty of fuel from you. But it's also to keep you from revealing the abuse to anyone in your circle and to make you more and more dependent on them.

In spite of your turning yourself into a complete doormat who bows down to their every whim, one day they just discard you, without a backward glance. You're left stranded on this island of isolation and you've become so broken and damaged by this person you no longer know who you are. You've burned all your bridges and there is no one to turn to.

This all might sound like scaremongering, but please believe me when I tell you, it's not. I hear stories like this all the time from women, in particular, who find a way to message me. Often, it's in secret and they are fearful of being caught and advise me they will be deleting the messages as soon as they've been read.

How to avoid the trap – my advice

The best way to avoid this is to NEVER abandon your family or friends in favor of a new romantic partner. Ask yourself why would you even think about doing that? Why would you trust the opinion of someone new in your life, against family or friends you have known forever? There should ALWAYS be room for both in any healthy relationship and if someone tries to limit your time with them, marginalize the relationship in any way, or cut them out of your life, see the big Red Flag waving in the wind. Make it a big fat 'Deal Breaker' and put it on your list.

But what if it's too late, and you've fallen into that trap and now find yourself isolated? What can you do then? One of the reasons I started my Facebook Groups was to help people who find themselves in this situation to be able to connect with other people who know what they are going through. If you're stuck in isolation now, come and join one of my groups. You're not alone! Set up a new Facebook profile and create a new Gmail account your partner doesn't know about.

I also recommend reaching back out to your family and those who were close friends and tell them what you've been through. They may not all welcome you with open arms, but the genuine ones, who truly do love you, will. Take the chance.

Get professional help. Find a therapist who understands NPD and abuse, to help you understand why this has happened to you, help you release the trauma and never let it happen to you again.

CHAPTER FIVE

THE BIG RED FLAGS OF NARCISSISTIC ABUSE
RED FLAG Nos 41-50

Now whilst all of the flags I've covered so far are vitally important to know about, my hope is by sharing them in this book, you'll know what to look for and how to avoid the traps, I want to bring home the reality of what this kind of abuse causes and why it is so emotionally, psychologically and physically damaging to you if you don't heed the warnings, or if, by the time you came to this book you were already knee-deep in narcissistic abuse.

The next 10 'Flags' are the big, bad wolves of narcissistic abuse. It does not take years for your life and your psyche, to be completely ruined by a Romantic Predator. It can happen in as little as a few months. Your entire reality will have changed and you will be in a mind-fog about what the hell has happened to you. You've been Love Bombed, Devalued, and Discarded. Everything you once held to be true has been shattered into pieces. Your confidence has gone, your self-worth is in tatters and your mental and physical health may be a major cause for concern.

Because of the nature of these BIG Red Flags, I'm not going to provide a separate 'How to avoid the traps – my advice' section as I have done with all the previous flags. If you're experiencing any of these big flags, avoidance is irrelevant. It's too late to avoid them because you are now deep in 'Narcland' and the abuse is deeply entrenched. I will, therefore, add commentary and advice where I feel it will be helpful along the way.

Red Flag No 41: Cognitive Dissonance

Cognitive dissonance came from American Social Psychologist Leon Festinger, and the theory is that we have this inner drive to hold all our attitudes and behavior in harmony to avoid disharmony or dissonance. When something gets in the way of that, we get cognitive inconsistency. What this means is when two conflicting things happen, your brain struggles to make sense of these two opposing things.

This happened to me once, many years ago, when a much-loved aunt accused me of stealing 400 pounds out of her handbag. I was so stunned, I remember feeling as if someone had died, the feeling of disbelief and shock was that intense. I just could not reconcile the aunt who I'd always loved and defended when other people made fun of her (because she often did or said really stupid things) and whom I believed always had one good trait; her judge of character, and the aunt who could possibly think I would go into her purse in the middle of the night and steal 400 pounds. I didn't speak to her for over 10 years and when I finally did, it was the day of my mother's funeral.

What happens in a narcissistic relationship is your partner is behaving one way in the beginning, and it's all wonderful, then suddenly their behavior changes and they become cruel and hurtful... and you don't understand what is going on. There are two things going on in your mind now that don't make sense: two conflicting realities you've experienced with this same person. There's a complete inability to reconcile two totally conflicting things in a way that makes sense. When your two worlds collide in this way and your brain is scrambling to make sense if it, this is cognitive dissonance.

Gaslighting is one of the main tactics leading to cognitive dissonance, because it makes you question your reality and start doubting yourself. Because it's so very subtle and the narcissist is so good at twisting and bending your reality, you start questioning yourself. Over time, you lose your grasp on reality and come to depend even more on your partner for validation. You become even more co-dependent.

What also happens is that you downplay the bad and recall the good, because this makes you feel better but it also lays the groundwork for more abuse to continue. This is how the cycle of abuse works. Your abuser sees that he or she has gotten away with some bad behavior because you're still there, you've forgiven them. They have free rein to do it again.

Unfortunately, the standard recommendations for dealing with cognitive dissonance are not very effective when you are going through the emotional turmoil of a narcissistic relationship because cognitive dissonance creates a FEELING in you... and by the time it happens, you're already in that feeling, reeling from the shock and there's nothing you can do to turn back the clock and change that. It's also very difficult to predict it and therefore, almost impossible to 'avoid'.

What you can do is look back at it and understand what it was, and why it happened. Understand it was not your fault, you didn't cause it to happen and there was nothing you could have done to prevent it or done differently to make it less painful. It's one of the many painful prices you will have to pay if you're in a relationship with a narcissist.

On the upside, once you realize it's happened the first time, it's not going to be quite as galling or shocking when it happens again, because the narcissist's pattern will usually become clear to you. They'll bounce around between devaluing, Love Bombing, devaluing, discarding and hoovering as they continue to play havoc with your emotions.

One of the most critical things you can do is ground yourself in reality. Grounding yourself requires that you tune into yourself and consider if you are feeling confused, upset or uncomfortable in any way, and if so why? What is going on in your mind/body that is causing the confusion? Previously, I talked about your feelings being your emotional barometer; what are they telling you now? Your body registers emotions and turns them into physical pain (see Red Flag No 44, coming up shortly) so it's vital you learn to listen in to yourself.

Write it down and connect with the reality of what is really going on, emotionally and physically, for you. If possible, call a trusted friend and talk to him/her about it. Talking about it can help you get clarity that you currently don't posses, but a friend does. These actions will help you validate what really happened and know you are NOT losing the plot. A narcissist just wants you to think you are! If you do these things, you will be far less likely to fall deeply down the cognitive dissonance rabbit hole.

But as I always advise, learn as much as you can about NPD, reach out for support, get a therapist and get the hell out of the relationship, because your sanity depends on it.

Red Flag No 42: Toxic Shame/Guilt

We all experience shame and guilt as these emotions are part of what makes us human. We've all done things we've felt bad about or regretted, and the function of guilt is to keep our moral compass pointed in the right direction. Usually it does the job quite well: we learn from our mistakes, forgive ourselves, vow never to do it again and move on.

Toxic shame and guilt, however, are entirely different and much more complicated emotions to deal with. Toxic shame develops in childhood, usually because of dysfunctional parents or caregivers, who raised you to believe you were deficient, not good enough and not worthy of love. As a young child, your developmental needs were not met and you were not allowed to express and learn about the world the way a 'normal' child would. If you accidentally spilled something, you would have been punished. If you wet the bed, you would have been punished, if you asked for a drink, or food, you would have been denied. You would have very soon internalized a belief that something was wrong with you, because as a child you did not have the critical faculty to understand it was your parents who were toxic and abusive, not you.

So sadly, you grow up with a completely distorted view of who you really are and what you deserve in this life. You spend your entire life trying to please others, and when it doesn't work (which of course it doesn't with a narcissist), you heap more shame and guilt upon yourself for being so inadequate. You may hate yourself for it. You may wish you'd never been born and the evil messages you've had programmed into you as a child - 'You're useless!', 'You're so stupid/fat/ugly/whatever' - continue to play over and over in your mind, reinforcing the negative belief you have about yourself.

It's easy to see why, when a narcissist comes along with all their charm and sunlight, you fall hook, line and sinker. Maybe this is the first time anyone has ever said anything nice to you or about you.

But as we know, this honeymoon period doesn't last, and the narcissist will already have figured out you are emotionally damaged. And they are going to hammer the nail in much more deeply. All of those feelings of guilt and shame you have about yourself will be reinforced afresh via this new person. But do you think 'Wow, he's/she's so nasty!'? No, you immediately turn the criticisms in on yourself, because you know you're to blame, you're no good, it must be your fault they are being mean and cruel. You are repeating a subconscious pattern you have unwittingly, unknowingly learned as a child. If you were also the 'Scapegoat Child' constantly compared against the 'Golden Child', this negative perception of yourself is going to run even deeper.

Toxic shame also makes it impossible for you to stand up for yourself. You've never learned that you had any rights as a child, so you don't believe you have any as an adult. This makes it so easy for a narcissist to swan in, sweep you off your feet and start pushing you back down where YOU believe you belong. You're a pre-programmed puppet, ready to dance to the new puppeteer's tune.

If you're suffering with this kind of shame pain, please know it is not you, it is not your fault and you don't deserve to go on living with this false construct of who you are. I urge you to find a therapist to help you work through it, release it, forgive yourself and learn to love yourself and fully heal. I want you to know it was NOT your fault. I can't emphasize that enough. You are not to blame.

Red Flag No 43: Trauma Bonding

One of the first questions a victim of narcissistic abuse is often asked after they reveal the depths of despair they were in during their relationship with a narcissist, is 'Why didn't you leave sooner' or worse, 'Why the hell did you go BACK?'

The answer is due to trauma bonding, a term first used by Patrick J. Carnes, Ph.D., who is the founder of the International Institute for Trauma and Addiction Professionals, and he outlined how traumatic bonding occurs as the result of ongoing cycles of abuse in which 'Intermittent Reinforcement' of reward and punishment creates powerful emotional bonds which are difficult to change.

Trauma bonding is also often referred to as Stockholm Syndrome, named after a very famous botched bank heist in Stockholm, where the hostages formed bonds with their captors and eventually refused to testify against them in court. When your life suddenly depends on another person or persons, how you view, react and feel about them changes because they hold your life in their hands.

Such theories of reward and punishment have their roots in classic behavioral psychology, and I remember B.F. Skinner and his rats' experiments when I was studying psychology. Skinner came up with 'Operant Conditioning' theory and his experiments showed – in very simple terms, if a rat pressed a lever and no food pellet was delivered immediately after the lever was pressed and none after several attempts, the rat would give up. But if a food pellet was delivered intermittently, the rat would keep pressing the lever. Basically, the idea that 'I might get a pellet this time', kept the motivation high to keep trying. Comparative studies show playing the slot machines functions the same way... the gambler will keep going and going in the hope that the win will happen.

When you are Trauma Bonded, you desperately want to go back to your abuser, even though you know they have made your life hell. The pull to go back is still tremendously powerful. The reason trauma bonding is so powerfully addictive and hard to break is because of the biochemicals in your brain. I'm going to do a very brief run through of those in case you're not familiar with this news!

Feelings of happiness comes from four happy chemicals and those are:

Oxytocin – also known as the 'love hormone'. This is released during touching, intercourse and orgasm. It's the same hormone that enables bonding between mother and child. So, during the 'Love Bombing' stage, there's very likely plenty of this being released in your brain.

Dopamine – the pleasure from eating, drinking, exercise and sex all release Dopamine. Addiction to alcohol or cocaine causes bursts of this to flood the system, which is why people become addicted to substances. The intense pleasure you experienced in the early stages with the narcissist has caused an addiction and you want that 'hit' again. You'll keep needing those rewards.

Dopamine is also now thought to be 'more related to anticipatory pleasure and motivation', according to my friend and fellow author, Som Bathla, in his book 'Build a Happier Brain: The Neuroscience and Psychology of Happiness (see Reading and Resources Section at the end of the book). What is also significant about this, as Bathla points out and what is significant if you think back to the love bombing stage, when you were excitedly awaiting the next text, email or call from your new lover, is the mere *anticipation* of these is releasing Dopamine so your system is being kept in a heightened state of arousal constantly in these early days of seduction.

This is also significant if you think about the ongoing narcissistic relationship dynamic. After the highs of 'Love Bombing, the 'Devaluing' follows, but narcissists typically swing back from time to time with flashes of the 'Love Bombing' to remind you of how great the 'Honeymoon' period was and that keeps you hanging on. Effectively, though being abusive most of the time, they are keeping you bonded to them with the vague notion things will go back to being the way they were in the 'Golden Period'.

And you, when you keep recalling that Golden Period, are creating a dopamine spike in your brain by your hope/anticipation that it will come back. And when it does, and the narcissist does something wonderful again, bang! This 'Intermittent Reinforcement' keeps you stuck in the relationship, hoping things will go back to the way they were. You've just had proof that the person you fell in love with is still there so you believe they will return to being that person all the time. But they never do.

Serotonin – this regulates mood, social behavior, appetite, sleep, memory and sexual function and it contributes to our overall happiness and wellbeing. During the early days, you'll have this chemical flooding your system. Low levels of Serotonin lead to depression and Selective Serotonin Reuptake Inhibitors (SSRIs) are the most commonly prescribed anti-depressants. (See Reading and Resource List at the end of the book).

Endorphins – our natural painkillers and anti-stress chemicals. This chemical can cause feelings of euphoria, loss of appetite and release of sex hormones.

When these four chemicals are working over time during the love bombing stage, you're up against a veritable army of love chemicals working on making you addicted and of course, these all play significant roles in the sexual chemistry, in addition to your personal, emotional feelings about this person. You don't stand a chance! It has often been said trauma bonding creates a dependency as difficult to break as alcohol or drug addiction. Those love-chemicals are firing on all four cylinders again, and your idea that this narcissist really loves and cares for you, if only they could just work stuff out... lodges in your head so firmly because you're craving that feeling of being in love. You want those happy chemicals!

There are three more that come into the fray!

Cortisol – regulates the 'fight or flight' response and during an abusive relationship, there is plenty of stress, but often no way to 'fight or flee' so that stress is kept in your body.

Adrenaline and Norepinephrine – are both connected to the fight or flight mechanism and released in stressful situations where 'fight or flight' might be required. So again, if you can't fight or flee, these chemicals are all being released but they are being prevented from doing their jobs and getting stuck in your body.

Testosterone – in men of course and regulates sex drive. When faced with a gorgeous, sexy person, it's going to be heading into overdrive!

There has been plenty of research to show prolonged stress is seriously damaging to your health, and if you consider the interplay of these chemicals in your body, is it any wonder? I will discuss health issues in Flag No 44.

Any kind of addiction is toxic and addiction to a narcissist is especially so, because it leads you down a path of behavior modification of yourself that's only happening because you want to keep the narcissist happy and you want those feelings of love and security back again. This is when the erosion of self, loss of self-esteem and self-love start kicking in. The narcissist is totally in control of you and your emotional merry-go-round. You're spinning in all directions and don't know which end is up anymore.

You start believing when things go wrong, it's your fault and you need to work harder at the relationship, you need to be better, you need to stop being the cause of his (or her) troubles. You start blaming yourself and trying really hard not to rock the boat. There is nothing you can do to NOT rock the boat, because narcissists crave stormy waters and they'll find a way to rock it. Before you know it, you'll be back in that place where you can't do or say anything right.

Having had dysfunctional or narcissistic parents, (Red Flag No 15), will also come into play because you've picked up the faulty subconscious programming which has you believing you're not good enough and you have to 'people please' to the nth degree in the hope that you will be accepted and loved. You won't be.

You might leave, because it has become unbearable... but that longing, that craving, to be back in the arms of the Narc is all consuming. Now you're like an addict without a fix, an alcoholic without a drink... you're so addicted to the narcissist you are helpless when they come crawling back in... and they will... it might take 20 years, but they'll come back if they can.

You might be the one to break 'No Contact' because the compulsion is too strong to resist. This tendency to go back to situations that trigger unresolved traumas from earlier in your life, (particularly childhood) is referred to as 'repetition compulsion', a term coined by the 'father of psychoanalysis', Sigmund Freud. There is a subconscious need to seek comfort in the familiar, even when that 'familiar' is abuse. Time and time again, victims go back to their abusers more than once before they finally break free.

It's also interesting to note that you can remain Trauma Bonded even if you've fallen out of love and despise your Ex. That chemical addiction is still working in your brain but emotionally it just adds to the confusion you are feeling.

Taking all these factors into account, is it any wonder breaking the trauma bond can be so incredibly difficult? How do you cure the deep, aching hole in your heart? Even long after you've left the relationship, that emotional pain will not go away and you wonder if you will ever feel whole and healed again?

I want you to know you CAN heal. It is possible and I've seen it happen time and time again with clients I've worked with. Clients who were feeling desperately unhappy, who were suffering with flashbacks and battling every day not to go back to their abuser. These clients were able to release deep traumatic pain and free themselves completely from the Trauma Bond, Flashbacks and Triggers. You can too!

In the meantime, please know it IS possible. You can get your life back, you can get your SELF back, and you can be happy again. You do NOT have to live with this horrible feeling of despair forever. Here are some tips that will help you (see also healing tips for Flag No 44):

Tip No 1

Go No Contact if you haven't already. This is critical. You need time and 'head space' to start connecting with your true self again and if you keep in touch with your abuser, you will keep yourself stuck in the negative loop and you always run the risk of being Hoovered back in. No Contact is a life-saver. If you can't do this because of co-parenting or business issues, Grey Rock as much as possible.

Tip No 2

Stop self-blaming. I've mentioned this many times in the book and it's important to remember it was not your fault. You are not to blame for being targeted, abused and victimized. You must let this truth become your own new belief and I want you to embrace it and hold onto the thought with as much passion as you can muster.

Tip No 3

When you start feeling all dewy-eyed about the 'love' you're craving and missing, hit the pause button in your head. Then change your position – if you're sitting down, stand up, if you're standing, sit down and so on. This creates a 'pattern interrupt' in your brain and helps you to stop letting your thoughts rule you. With the button on pause, bring to mind the reality of what the relationship has or had become. Recall with as much detail as you can how much the Narc has hurt you. Really think about this. Call up as many incidents as you can imagine. See that person for who they really are deep down.

Tips No 4

Now ask yourself if you really want to go back to that reality? Ask yourself if someone who really loved you would treat you in such a manner? Think about what LOVE really is – what does love really mean to you, when you get down to the core of it? Examine closely the aspects of abuse that caused you to leave in the first place and ease yourself out of denial. Be brutally honest with yourself and top trying to pretend they were anything other than what they really are; A narcissist who hurt, manipulated, gaslighted, cheated, lied and betrayed you.

Tip No 5

I've also mentioned grief before and it's also important to remember you need to honor your feelings and grieve for the loss. Spend a little time acknowledging and accepting whatever feelings come up for you. Accept that you are human and you are hurting but tell yourself 'This too shall pass'. Because it will. If you stay No Contact or keep Grey Rocking, you'll feel more in control. With time you will heal.

Tip No 4

Get out and about and DO things. Take long walks. Go to the gym, cinema, shopping mall, or take a nice walk in nature. Just get out and about rather than wallowing in misery at home. Make yourself do it.

Tip No 5

Take a few moments to breathe and imagine a stress-free, narc-free future for yourself. Really visualize how that would look and feel for you. Remember, creative visualization is powerful and you can activate the Law of Attraction by focusing on what you want in your future, not what you don't. Affirm that you have taken a giant step to heal yourself and feel proud of that. Give yourself a hug and praise yourself.

Tip No 6

Keep positive by telling yourself you can and will get over this. Find a phrase that signifies a happy, Narc-free future for yourself and repeat it over in your head every time you start thinking thoughts which make you feel miserable.

Tip No 7

Reach out and get support. If you've been in a narcissistic relationship for a long time, the chances are very high that you've become isolated, because that is what a narcissist does. They work to ensure they isolate you from your family and friends and you could be feeling very alone and lost. You don't have to be. Come and join my Facebook Group (I have one for women only and one for men only – links at the end of the book). Connect with me and the other women in the group who know what you are going through. Just realizing that you are not alone and meeting others who understand can be immensely helpful.

Tip No 8

Consider getting therapy. Most of the women I know who have recovered reached out and got therapy to help them understand and get over the abuse. If you can't fight this alone, please get in touch. If you are really struggling with trauma bonding, you can email me to apply for a private session to discuss how I can help you. Take the first big step to healing.

This is by no means an exhaustive explanation about trauma bonding or ways to heal from it, but these simple tips can help you to give yourself the reality check you need to keep you away from the narc and you will get stronger the more you practice these techniques. Remember you owe it to yourself to find YOU again and you must not give up.

Red Flag No 44: Narcissistic abuse is ruining your health

Before I get into this, I will say if you are suffering any kind of physical symptoms or think you might be suffering with any of the things mentioned in this post, always be sure to see your doctor. I'm not a medical practitioner and I'm not qualified to give any kind of medical advice. I am, however, a certified Clinical NLP/Hypnotherapist with experience helping people to recover from trauma and abuse.

Unfortunately, any kind of stress, even in an average relationship, can have extremely severe consequences for your health. But narcissistic abuse takes it to another level. In a post by Harvard Health Publishing School, Robert H. Schmerling, MD, explained what stress is and if you think back to the part about your brain's chemicals, you'll connect the dots here.

What is Stress?

"A common definition of "stress" is any experience that causes tension, whether physical, psychological, or emotional, especially if it sets off the "fight or flight" response during which the adrenal gland releases adrenaline, leading to rapid pulse and breathing, and increased blood pressure. This serves us well if chased by a lion. But it's theorized that persistent stress (such as worry about finances, mental or physical health, or interpersonal relationships) could lead to chronic disease such as high blood pressure or autoimmune disease."

I'll put the link to his article in the Reading and Resources Section.

A vast amount of research has been carried out on stress, abuse and their effects on the body, and these examples are typically what you might feel when exposed to long-term doses:

- Confusion (cognitive dissonance)
- Betrayal
- Hopelessness
- Shame

·   Extreme disappointment

This emotional toll can also result in behavioral and physical side effects. You may experience:

·   Difficulty concentrating (dissociation)
·   Moodiness
·   Nightmares/Insomnia
·   Various aches and pains
·   Depression
·   Feeling worthless/useless, and hopeless
·   Feeling isolated and as if nobody can understand you

Anxiety related symptoms such as

·   Racing heartbeat
·   Muscle tension
·   Sweating
·   Shaking
·   Headaches, dizziness, chest pains

Sustained abuse over time will also lead to Complex-PTSD and examples are:

·   Angry outbursts when away from your abuser
·   Inability to control your emotions – crying a lot or unexpectedly
·   Being easily startled
·   Constant negative, fearful thoughts
·   Inability to trust anyone
·   Insomnia and nightmares
·   Reliving the trauma (flashbacks) and experiencing physical symptoms such as   those associated with any anxiety and/or panic attack
·   Inability to speak or function

· Persistent desire to return to your abuser if you've left (trauma bonding).

And in extreme cases, if left untreated, C-PTSD - can result in suicide, self-harming or self-medicating with drugs or alcohol to cope, which often leads to further problems with addiction.

All these symptoms of trauma persist even AFTER you've left the relationship. They can and will persist until you get help to deal with them. If you're suffering long-term with narcissistic abuse and get no help... you bottle up your emotions and they fester... and fester... and things get worse and worse for you, psychologically and physically.

This is what can and very often does lead to much more serious illness because when you are living in a constant state of hyper-arousal – and not the good kind - I'm talking about walking on eggshells, not knowing from one minute to the next what your partner is going to say or do. There's a constant stream of adrenaline flowing through your veins. Your nerves are constantly on edge, your body is not functioning the way it's meant to, you're constantly living on a knife-edge and your body starts to break down due to the prolonged stress overload. This type of stress is what can and does lead to cancer, heart attacks, hypertension and a host of autoimmune diseases. And I reiterate – these symptoms do NOT just go away once you get out of the relationship. There are two reasons:

One is because the body has learned to live in this constant state of stress, almost as if it has become normal for you, but it is not normal to live like this. The constant barrage of verbal abuse changes the neural pathways in your brain – completely distorting what you once held to be true about yourself.

Two is, in the case of childhood narcissistic or sexual abuse, you are subconsciously reinforcing the deeply held beliefs you have about your true value and worth. It is a chemical and emotional cocktail that's devastating to your emotional and physical health.

And there's more bad news. Recent research has now proven long-term narcissistic abuse can cause brain damage. This research has shown repeated emotional abuse causes the hippocampus, which is responsible for memory and learning, to shrink. Additionally, it causes the amygdala, which is where fear, grief, envy and shame live, to enlarge. Your brain is radically altered and you'll suffer with all those symptoms because of the overactive amygdala. I have had many women tell me they have trouble remembering things now.

The amygdala is also involved with the fight or flight mechanism, so triggers, flashbacks or painful memories can pop up, causing anxiety, panic attacks or avoidance behavior.

Not only that, a study by Psychology Professor Ethan Kross, of the University of Michigan, showed brain circuitry for physical pain and emotional pain are the same, so even if you are not being physically abused, the emotional pain is registering in your body the same way.

You know the fight, flight or freeze options... you're damned with a narcissist, whichever you choose on any given day of the week. You can't second guess what they want you to do or say, because whatever you do or say, it'll be wrong and they'll denigrate you for it. One of the reasons I believe the Grey Rock technique can be so effective is because it helps you to avoid being automatically corralled into the 'fight, flight or freeze' responses. By thinking ahead and planning your 'relaxed, non-responsive' attitude, you put yourself in much more control of your emotions and your body.

Here are some examples women in my FB Group have shared with me on how they believe narcissistic abuse has impacted their health:

Nervous breakdown…

"I got to the point of a nervous breakdown, ended up in hospital from concussion I caused myself for feeling I deserved to be punished. I actually fled to Oz to get away. I'm doing better but still I recognize how fragile my body is."

I've felt suicidal…

'I often feel anxious, have low self-esteem and depression. At times I've even felt suicidal. I also suffer with Rheumatoid arthritis.'

Racing heart, depression, insomnia and paranoia…

'I didn't realize how much confidence and self-esteem I had lost – I used to be so outgoing too! After escaping, I was depressed, anxiety-ridden, and in so much agony and despair to my core - all things I hadn't experienced before. Work helped pull me out of a lot of my fog, but CBD oil and 5HTP helped with the racing heart, depression, insomnia and paranoia - especially when out and about. (My Dr. approved this, as my cortisol was SO high). A lot of that is better, but I still take them because I still have moments of sadness and when I mention his name or talk about things (he gets sentenced Mon-fingers crossed*), it can get to me. Staying busy helps keep me outta my head too. I have freedom and I'm healing!'

*This woman's husband stabbed her in a fit of narcissistic rage. The wound required 13 stitches. She finally had enough and had him arrested.

I was bed-ridden for 3 months…

'My anxiety was so bad at one time that I had horrible rib cage pain. Had to have CT's, bone scan and blood work and doctors couldn't figure it out. I was bed ridden for three months total. It was

my mind saying that's enough. It's called I believe ribcage stress syndrome.* In a nutshell I was on the verge of having a nervous breakdown. I left my Narc six months ago after a 28-year marriage. I'm in counseling because of horrible anxiety and depression.'

*Costochondritis or Tietze's Syndrome

Constant panic attacks...

'This week I have had constant panic attacks! I was so full of anxiety that my body shut down yesterday and resulted in a migraine and I couldn't function! He resurfaced after a decade and it is like I am right back there again!'

Fibromyalgia...

'Fibromyalgia has plagued me for years. I feel like I will never be well again.'

Chronic Migraines...

'Chronic Migraines and Tension Headaches for 24 years. I feel it's trapped trauma from past childhood physical and mental abuse, rape... and then physical, financial, and narc abuse from ex-spouses.'

I have gone through self-harm...

'I have gone through self-harm, extreme anxiety and depression, I'm not sleeping, in constant pain, flashbacks.'

Feeling invisible...

'PTSD, anxiety, depression, breast pain and vitiligo. 5 years living with him and I am now completely white - I lost all the pigment in my skin. I account that to feeling invisible.'

I thought he was going to kill me…

'I have PTSD and chronic insomnia/ flipped sleep schedule from staying up all night watching him. I thought he was going to kill me. It hasn't flipped back since. It's been about a year and a half since I've left. The smallest things off the beaten track cause high anxiety nowadays and it was never like this before. I panic about simple things like going to the dentist or certain events that are just recreational with friends. A lot of anxiety.'

Anxiety, low self-esteem…

'Anxiety, low self-esteem, intrusive thoughts, self-worth issues, low energy and fibromyalgia.'

Chronic depression, bruxism…

'Chronic pain, chronic depression, bruxism. Hyperventilate. Poor self-esteem, stolen memories. Cruel, mean, debasing, demeaning, controlling. Unable to make a decision.'

So, you see, all these people attribute these symptoms to the stress of being in narcissistic relationships. The truth is, it does affect your mental and physical health.

Tips to help with healing

What can be difficult for anyone suffering physically and mentally is connecting the dots between their physical symptoms and the abuse, so it's important for you to take a personal inventory by looking back over your life, from childhood onwards. If there is a history of dysfunctional parents and toxic relationships, it's important you start making the connection. Write it all down. It might seem obvious to you, but I've talked to many people who discuss their illness and their toxic relationships as though there is

NO connection whatsoever. When they start really digging deep, they begin to see their relationships are the cause of their illness. This first step of writing it all down can help you to start seeing the pattern and connecting the dots. Just figuring this out for yourself can be very empowering because it can give you greater motivation to get out, or get healed.

In spite of how bad it might seem, there IS good news. Healing IS possible, starting with our brain. Much research in neuroscience has proven the brain can repair itself, thanks to neuroplasticity. The hippocampus can regenerate itself. Regular self-care is absolutely vital to get your brain back in top gear. It's important that you start taking care of yourself. You need to nourish and strengthen your emotional core, because it has taken a massive hammering.

Here are some recommendations to help you get started on your healing journey and getting your mind and body back on track. Activities such as these are said to increase the all-important Dopamine levels in your brain and though I'm putting them here in the health part, I recommend these healing tips across the board, so even if you are still physically healthy, don't neglect the all-important mental, psychological and emotional healing because you need it and these tips will help.

Here they are:

Guided Meditation – studies from Harvard University show the brain can be repaired with just 27 minutes a day practicing mindfulness. The study showed a major increase in the density of both the hippocampus and amygdala, as well as reduction in stress. If you think meditation is too flaky or airy-fairy for you, think again. Start practicing daily. There are tons of great free choices on YouTube.

Eat a healthy, nutritional diet – a recent TEDx Talk I watched showed how diet affects age-related memory and Alzheimer's. The amygdala is, of course, affected so it's worth considering changing your diet to include 'brain health' foods. I've long believed that our diet also has a huge impact on our health, (I've been vegetarian for 30 years) so I definitely recommend researching the mind-body-food connection. I will put the link to that talk in the Resources Section at the end.

Get out in nature - walking in nature and fresh air are vital for your health, as is sunshine. If you live in a country where there is not much sun or you get long depressing dark winters, like you do in the UK, consider getting a light therapy box (widely used to treat Seasonal Affective Disorder – SAD – see Reading and Resources Section). If you don't live where there is access to nature walks, go to the local park.

Exercise – any kind of exercise is going to benefit you. Get back into the gym, go swimming, hiking or join a Yoga class. Find an exercise you enjoy and can look forward to.

Do crosswords/Sudoku/Jigsaws – engage your brain in something interesting/ challenging but not stressful. This will help take your mind off your worries, literally.

Listen to music – music is one of the best tools you can use to instantly change your mood and uplift yourself. Get some rousing tunes on, get off your butt and dance! Do this even if you don't feel like it. Your brain will respond to the music if you just give it the chance. Just don't play any songs that remind you of your Ex.

Pray – Do you believe in a power bigger than yourself, something far greater than you? The majority of people do. A Lifeway Poll showed that 31% of Americans pray several times a day, 48% at least once a day, and 65% at least once a month. Another Pew study showed that 'More than 1 in 5 of those who pray daily were religiously unaffiliated'. Whether you believe in God, traditional religion, or some other higher power, if you DO believe in something, and you have faith, use it. Praying can be incredibly comforting and gives you hope in desperate times.

Volunteer – this is one of the easiest and best ways to get out of your own head because it forces you to think about the problems other people (or animals) are having. Volunteering has been shown to have multiple benefits for YOU as well as the organization you are contributing your time to. Some of those are: Make new friends, develop new job skills, make a difference in the world and feel immediately more worthwhile. You'll also be valued and appreciated, you'll have somewhere to go, people to meet and something to look forward to. Most importantly, you'll feel good about yourself. So look around your community and see who's looking for help. Thrift Stores and Animal Shelters especially, will almost always welcome you with open arms.

Journal – if you enjoy writing, get it down on paper. Writing is cathartic and it also gets the emotions out of your head and onto the page. Many people in my network have turned their experience of abuse into books. This helps with their healing, awakens them to a different, deeper purpose for their lives and helps/inspires others who read their stories. (See Reading and Resources for some recommendations) Do you have a potential book in you? If yes, start writing. If not, write anyway because it's therapeutic for you. You may discover a hidden talent for writing, as did my friend and author of Dating Harley Quinn, Lee Miller, whose work I quoted earlier in the book. Lee's experience with a narcissist propelled him to write the book and he now has over 2 million views on his Quora answers on various aspects of narcissistic abuse and recovery. No one is more shocked that Lee himself!

Get creative – if you enjoy art or crafts of any kind or had a hobby you loved but gave up on, get back into them. Doing something creative can be immensely helpful because it will bring you back to simple joy you will have forgotten about. Also tapping into your creative center takes your focus away from your pain and gives your mind a much-needed break from the constant downer.

Laughter – you may have forgotten how to laugh because your life has been so full of pain, but find something to laugh at. Research shows laughter activates the reward center of the brain and releases dopamine. Make the time to watch a funny movie, or a comedian or remember things that really made you laugh. If you can get together with family or friends for some fun and laughter, do it. You need to remind yourself that there are still joyful things in life worth fighting for.

Get a therapist – if you're in a position to invest in a therapist, absolutely do this. A skilled therapist can help you deal with the trauma, release it and take back control of your life. I know this because I see it happening with my clients all the time. And it doesn't have to take years to accomplish. I use NLP/Hypnotherapy/Inner Child Healing and the results I've helped my clients achieve have been absolutely stunning. I've helped them clear the Trauma Bond in ONE session. It might sound impossible but it's not. The deep trauma you have eating your insides up can be released in as little as one session and it's lasting and permanent. I've helped clients end crippling panic attacks, depression, C-PTSD, flashbacks and triggers, but most importantly, I've helped them find themselves again and start loving themselves! You CAN heal and I want you to believe that.

Pick one (or more) of the above as a starting point and MAKE yourself do it. You want to heal. You need to heal. And finally, no matter where you are now in your journey with narcissistic abuse, have faith and hope, and BELIEVE that you can heal. Because you CAN.

Red Flag No 45: Discarded like trash

I've heard this expression so many times, I thought I'd use it here to drive the point home that this is how you will end up if you get involved with a narcissist. It is such a horrible thing to say or think of when it's about a human being, but that is how a narcissist makes you feel when they discard you. Like a piece of trash they no longer want or need.

Narcissists walk out on you even after years together, they leave marriages and children behind, whilst making it clear they have found someone else and how happy they are. They will twist the knife by making sure you know this. They will flaunt it whenever they can, because discarding you is not enough for them. They want to continue hurting you. The reality that they can just walk away from you after years, after professing to love you so much, is one of the hardest things for the victim to come to terms with. They simply cannot believe it. It's just too much to contemplate. How can they do this? I get asked this question at least once a day. And the answer is simple: they can do it because they are narcissists. They have a mental illness.

They'll do this even if you're financially dependent on them and they'll strive to take everything from you and leave you penniless, in the gutter. If you take legal action (which you must do!), they will fight you every step of the way.

If you're getting divorced or there are custody issues with children, a narcissist will do everything in their power to make things as difficult as possible. They don't want a peaceful, easy settlement that's best for everyone. No, that would be what a normal person wants, so if you're going to be divorcing, brace yourself because a whole new fight is about to begin and you're in for the battle of your life. At this stage, you need all the help you can get and you need to find a lawyer who knows their way around NPD and abuse. This isn't going to be easy, but they can be found.

Even if you win, don't expect them to comply with court orders, for child support or other financial obligations. Remember, narcissists don't recognize authority and they consider themselves above the law, so be ready for that when it happens. Because it very possibly will happen.

What almost everyone I've talked to about this struggle with most relates to their complete shock about how they feel. How could their partner just walk away, as if they had never meant anything to them? As they begin researching and learning about NPD and abuse, they are shocked even more at the realization of what they have been dealing with. You discover the person you loved, who you thought loved you, is a total fake and it's devastating. How can anyone treat another human being this way? It's incomprehensible to you. The cognitive dissonance really kicks in here because you simply can't accept this. Initially you just reject it because it just CAN'T be true. This is unimaginably difficult when you have been living with someone for so long – even 20 or more years, before one day they just walk out. But as you learn more and start connecting all the dots in your relationship, the truth slowly dawns on you.

With that comes the total emotional fallout. You are left devastated, feeling like a fool – how could you have been taken in? How could you have fallen for it? How can you ever forgive yourself for your own stupidity? How can you ever trust anyone again? How the f*** are you going to deal with this excruciating pain? These and many more questions, will be tumbling around inside your head as your shattered heart tries to make sense if it all.

It is not a pleasant place to be – it's complete hell. On top of all this hurt, confusion and emotional pain, comes depression, to the point that you struggle to get out of bed in the morning, anxiety, C-PTSD and trauma bonding, which you don't understand – how can you want them back after what they've done to you? Why do you miss them? You may feel anger, hatred and want to exact revenge, get in front of your Ex and give them a piece of your mind. You might find yourself creating alternative profiles on SM so you can stalk them and see what they are up to. Doing this will just hurt more because you'll see them with their new flame, they'll be looking happy, (out on a boat YOU paid for with your life savings!) while you are struggling to put the broken pieces of yourself back together.

You'll be going out of your mind trying to figure out WHY? Why have they done this when you've done everything in your power to please them? When you've loved them without question? When you've given up and given in on everything they wanted and needed? When you supported them through any number of their difficult times? What have you done wrong?

The simple truth is, **you've done nothing wrong.** Your only mistake was having the misfortune to hook up with them in the first place. But you couldn't have known what you were letting yourself in for. You didn't know then what you know now. The reason the narcissist discards you is based purely on the complex psychology of their disorder – not on anything you did or didn't do. You must believe this.

Remember they idealized you in the beginning and as long as you keep compliant and keep giving them the fuel they need, they will stay with you. During this time they will undoubtedly be getting fuel from other sources, but you may not ever be aware of this. They can idealize you for a long time, but gradually they start to realize you are not perfect. You're a real human being with real needs, and they can't cope with that. In their minds you exist purely to satisfy their wants, needs and their idealized version of you. When reality starts to butt in too much, they flee. Because they don't know how to deal with 'real' relationships. Everything about them is an illusion. They are an illusion you fell for and you are an illusion they targeted because they thought you were the magical, mystical being, the ideal love, mythologized in their minds – a creature fabricated out of their own ridiculous fantasies.

But, of course, you're just an ordinary human being. In their warped minds, YOU have let them down. You have betrayed them – by not being perfect. By not living up to their fantasy. By not being compliant. They feel they have a right to pay you back for letting them down – and that's why they start the Smear Campaign (coming up shortly) against you. Remember their logic is their logic and it doesn't make any sense to anyone else. They bear no blame for anything in the relationship because, as you now know, they cannot take responsibility for their actions and blame-shift constantly. Nothing is ever their fault, so the break-up is always your fault and you're going to be punished. They will see to it.

You must also realize the Discard actually starts as soon as the Devaluing starts. It's just the finale to the years of Devaluing you've endured. It's just a matter of time. The narcissist will discard you based on their notion of your blatant imperfections, but what it boils down to is this:

You've stopped giving them the fuel they need and there is nothing to gain from staying with you. It could be for any of these reasons:

- You've got Grey Rock down to such a fine art they get no response from you = no fuel. Even when you know they've been abusive and that's why you've 'Grey Rocked' them, the reality of them leaving still hits hard.

- You're so emotionally and physically exhausted you can't be bothered to react or respond anymore = no fuel.

- You've seen through them and they know it. This is the most terrifying thing that can happen to them and they cannot face the truth of who they are, so they will leave you as punishment, and they will continue trying to destroy you.

- Or, it could be and often is, they have found a superlative new source of supply and they want to immediately dedicate their all to that new person.

This last one can come totally out of the blue. There you were, ambling along and thinking everything in your life was fine, your relationship was going to go on as far as you were concerned and suddenly this emotional tornado blows through your life and you don't know what has hit you. This kind of 'unexpected discard' is horrendously painful. Your plans of a lifetime together, of 'happily ever after' have blown up in smoke and you're left choking on the fumes.

To add insult to massive injury, they immediately start posting pictures on SM so you can see them looking all shiny and happy with their new target. You'll start obsessing about this person – what do they have that you don't? Why have they been chosen? What's wrong with you? Why weren't you enough? You may find yourself feeling absolute hatred for this person you don't even know because you view them as the one who has stolen your man or woman. If you feel this way, it's not unusual. You need to channel your anger and hurt somewhere, but when you calm down, you will realize the new target is not and never was, the problem. And you are not and never were, the problem. Your partner is the problem.

Regardless of the why, you're left in a crumpled heap, shattered, broken and struggling to fathom the unfathomable.

When this happens to you, you NEED to get support. Contact family or friends who will believe you. Get into a support group. Get a therapist if you can. If you can't, contact a support helpline. Most areas have them if you look them up. Though this will feel like the worst time in your life, tell yourself you will get over this. Just say it and keep repeating it like a mantra in those early days. You have to dig deep and find every ounce of courage you can to fight your way out of this. But you CAN get over it. You can. You can. You can.

Even if you are the one doing the discarding your life doesn't suddenly change and go back to being normal. You'll never be the same person again. The trauma you've been through will have changed you forever. If you are the one who has discarded the narcissist because you've finally woken up and realized you cannot spend another minute in the relationship, get ready for more trouble, because it's coming.

I just want to mention there are some cases where the narcissist refuses to leave. This may be because they are sitting pretty and content to keep it that way. It may be financially better for them, maybe they're happy to have their clothes laundered, meals cooked, home kept spotless... this is much more likely to happen with a vulnerable narcissist who is too lazy to find another situation and is quite happy to carry on using you as his or her personal servant. In this case, if you're ready for this to be over, you may have to take legal action.

No matter how the relationship ends, trouble, as I said, is coming up, in the shape of the next two flags.

Red Flag No 46: Flying Monkeys come out in force

Whether you've been discarded or were the one discarding, you need to be aware of these nasty critters. Of course, they are people but I suggest you start thinking of them as nasty little critters who need to be swatted away like bugs. Reduce them to that in your mind and don't give them any power over you. You may well have encountered them during your relationship because they do show up, but it's during the Discard phase they are most dangerous and come out of the woodwork.

The term comes from those nasty characters the Wicked Witch of the West had flying around doing her dirty work for her in the movie 'The Wizard of Oz'. They are the allies a narcissist 'recruits' to use against you in their Smear Campaigns. It's an expansion of the narcissist's ability to abuse you – basically, abuse by proxy. Narcissists are very creative in their use of flying monkeys and they may also use them in their triangulation and hoovering campaigns.

There are different types of flying monkeys: Nasty and Naïve

Nasty Monkeys

On the nasty side, if they are particularly virulent or even narcissists themselves, they'll spread lies, rumors and gossip about you. They'll reveal secrets or personal information they shouldn't even be in possession of and that they have absolutely no right to reveal, but they don't care.

They will do that on SMor anywhere they can get anyone to listen. They'll be nasty and abusive when you meet them and try to make you feel worthless – and if you've discarded the narc, you'll be painted a complete witch. They're likely to be just as toxic and nasty as the narcissist is and because they've bonded with your Ex for whatever reason - maybe they want the status, maybe they just enjoy being nasty for its own sake – matters not. One thing is for sure, they are toxic and you don't want them anywhere near you.

Flying Monkeys

Then there are the naïve flying monkeys. These are people who have fallen for the charming façade most narcissists are so good at putting on. They genuinely think the narcissist is a good, nice, decent person, so when they start spinning their web of lies about you or playing the role of the victim, - something you can expect from them – the naïve monkey soaks it all up and thinks you're the crazy one or the heartless one who dumped or cheated on their friend or, they fall for the 'pretend concern' about you that the narcissist is feeding them (which happens during hoovering).

Recently, one of the members of my group mentioned how her Ex had sent one of his friends to persuade her to get back with him. They show up 'nice', but they are there, knowingly or otherwise, to do the narcissist's dirty work. Although these types won't go all out on character assassination of you, they still belong in the enemy camp because you can't trust them. The Narc might use them to find out what you're up to and report back to them. During the Discard phase, they will of course believe everything the narcissist says and they'll spread that knowledge around, believing it to be true.

How to deal with Flying Monkeys – 10 Tips that Work

1. Go 'No Contact' with everyone associated with your Ex-Narc.
2. Trust no one but those you know deep in your heart you can trust.
3. Warn people who know and like you that the Ex-Narc will be spreading lies about you.
4. Keep away from any places where you might run into any flying monkeys.
5. Ground yourself in your reality, you know the truth.
6. Don't react if you do come face-to-face (or online). Walk away. Don't engage. Delete. Block.
7. Consider moving – house, State or Country. People do it all the time, why couldn't you?
8. Get a therapist who is experienced in healing and recovery from narcissistic abuse.
9. Join a support group
10. Remember you are NOT helpless and your actions speak louder than words.

The best way to protect yourself from flying monkeys is to follow those 10 tips. No 6 is particularly important. If you do run into them, resist the urge to engage, defend yourself or tell the truth about the narcissist, because frankly, it'll fall on deaf ears and will only reinforce the lies your Ex is spreading about you. Ignore them and walk away, because they are not interested in the truth, and anything you do say will get straight back to your Ex and give them fuel. You can at least deprive them of that.

Red Flag No 47: Smear Campaigns

This is another horrendous nail in the coffin of your relationship. Narcissists are not content to end the relationship and walk away. They are so evil they have to emotionally eviscerate you in public because this gives them fuel and it validates them to other people who believe you were the crazy one who made their life hell. It's their kind of 'closure' - except, it's not always, because they often come back to Hoover you. There is no end to the lies they will tell and you have to be prepared for absolutely anything, because narcissists are completely unconscionable.

They do this because you dared to question them, to let them down, to not be the paragon of perfection they fabricated you to be or fantasized you to be in the first place. They have a pathological need to punish you for daring to see through them, for being so ordinary and human you caused their mask to slip and fall off. You have dared to expose them to themselves and they cannot allow this. They must do everything in their power now to discredit you and save their fake self from public exposure. They must destroy you and garner sympathy from anyone who will listen.

This is where the flying monkeys also get to work in earnest. You're not only up against the lies your Ex is telling about you all around town and across SM, you're up against the flying monkey brigade too. The main reason the narcissist embarks on a smear campaign is very much in sync with their standard behavior and there are three key reasons why they do it:

1) To destroy you. They want to discredit you to anyone who is still left in your circle, if they haven't isolated you from them.
2) To get their all-important fuel. Seeing you hurt privately and then publicly brings them joy. And yes, that is sick.
3) To protect themselves and their new source of supply. They will not want their new squeeze to hear about their abusive behavior so painting you as the crazy, jealous Ex will ensure that. Think back to Red Flag No 11 and how they talked to you about their ex. That's how they will have been talking about you during their love bombing of the new source.

Narcissists are sneaky, to put it mildly. They don't just spring this Smear Campaign out of the blue as soon as they discard you. No, they're too clever for that. Months beforehand, they will have started dropping subtle hints into the right ears, casting doubts on your state of mind, integrity, honesty and character in general. These might seem quite innocuous to the listener – a comment such as 'It's funny isn't it, how you can think someone is so amazing and then one day find out they're anything but.' They'll offer no more information, even if pressed, but this leaves the person who's heard it wondering. Even though no names have been mentioned and you've not been implicated, when the Discard bomb explodes and the Smear Campaign starts, people who have heard those comments will remember them being said and put two and two together. This is the typical type of subtle manipulation the narcissist uses.

In the case that you discard them, this can cause a massive narcissistic injury and incite narcissistic rage. You have dared to pull their mask off and expose them for what they are. They may, in this case, do everything in their power to persuade you to stay. They may Love-Bomb you like they did in the beginning. They will beg, plead, get down on their knees and cry and promise to change, get therapy, do whatever it takes, but this will all be lies and you know it. You must refuse. Refuse in your heart and soul to believe their lies. They may start stalking, harassing or threatening you, rubbing your face in their new supply and of course, the Smear Campaign is going to be epic.

Narcissistic Injury and Narcissistic Rage

It is not difficult to cause a 'narcissistic injury' to a narcissist, because their egos are both massive and extremely fragile. They will take deep offence if you say anything that paints them in a less-than-perfect light. It could be something completely innocuous, such as 'Maybe you could work on improving that', that could cut deep into their ego. In doing so you have threatened their sense of power and control and they will want to punish you for this. By saying anything that threatens their fake persona or not letting them get their own way, be the center of attention or asking them to be accountable for any kind of unacceptable behavior, you're causing a narcissistic Injury. They will not forgive, they will not forget. When it comes to Smear Campaigns, if you have discarded them, you have committed the worst crime possible against them. They will want revenge and the Smear Campaign against you will be vicious.

Narcissistic rage comes in many different forms. You can have the screaming, ranting, raving hysterics, when the narcissist throws a complete fit of rage and it can result in your being physically attacked or having your property smashed into pieces, but it can also be cold, silent, deadly rage. If you're even in a situation where you feel in danger of assault, get out if you can and call the police.

But back to the Smear Campaign. Remember narcissists have no respect for other people's boundaries so it's open season on anyone in your life they can reach. Their vicious lies can cost you family, friends and even your career. In the vilest cases, you can find yourself facing criminal charges for something you didn't do. This can happen with custody battles where they accuse you of child abuse and you end up in court trying to defend yourself against these lies. It happens more than I care to admit.

What can you do in the face of such character assassination? There are several things you can do to take back a measure of control.

Resist the urge to retaliate and defend yourself. Rein yourself in and realize reacting with anger and outrage is just going to give them a massive dose of feel-good fuel. You need to take a deep breath – or several – and ground yourself in YOUR reality. You know the truth and for the time being, that's all that matters.

If it's a custody or court battle, get all your legal ducks in a row and present the facts and everything you can supply to back it up, and let your lawyer do the fighting for you. If you have to show up in court, bring a family member or friend with you – don't 'go it alone'.

Pick and choose the family and friends who will believe you. Even if you think there is no one, you might be surprised to find there are. If they are true friends, they will know you are telling the truth and if they don't they are not your friends. Let them go.

Talk to your boss/HR Department and advise them of what's happening and to expect to hear lies about you.

Get out for real! You may have to take other radical steps to protect yourself, like moving house, State or Country. I know plenty of people who have done it.

Tell yourself you will get through this. Hold on to that thought.

Decide that you don't give a flying f*** about what other people think. Decide you're done with pretending and people-pleasing. Decide from now on, you're going to take care of yourself. Decide you are better than this and you deserve a whole lot better in your life. If you can do this and really FEEL it, you will reach a level of self-empowerment that will astound you.

Self-Love/Self-Care: Revisit the Tips to healing section of Flag No 44.

Get support/therapy. I've said this several times, but it's important to reach out to get the help and support you need. Know that you are NOT alone and there are people who can help you.

Don't let the Smear Campaign destroy you. Make it your mission to rise like a Phoenix from the ashes and take back your power.

Red Flag No 48: Hoovering – The Romantic Predator strikes again!

Vacuum Cleaners, aka Hoovers, suck up dust and debris. The term 'hoovering' is used to describe a common tactic the narcissist uses after the Discard phase, usually in multiple attempts to 'suck' you back into the relationship. These attempts bring the Romantic Predator fully back into play. They'll show up with fresh flowers and a fresh Love Bombing' campaign, pleas for forgiveness and promises to change. But underneath all this bullshit, it's the same old narcissist who hasn't changed at all. To them, you're nothing more than dust and debris that needs to be hoovered up and spat back out again when they're done abusing you a second - or more - times around.

You might think this is a preposterous idea when they've treated you like dirt – treated you like someone they hated, discarded you like trash, tried to destroy you, ruin you financially, left you emotionally bruised and battered... but none of this matters to a narcissist. What they've done – no matter how reprehensible – is of no consequence to them. Remember, they don't think like most people. Normal logic just isn't part of their make-up. The Romantic Predator shows up again and in spite of everything they've done to you and you fall right back into their trap. This is because you are still Trauma Bonded to them. You can't help it and you'll keep going back unless you get help to break the bond, so I highly recommend you get professional help to break that debilitating, life-sucking bond once and for all.

Again, the question is why? Why do they want you back when they've treated you to horrendous abuse and brutally discarded you? They do it for fuel, as in everything they do is to get fuel and they do it because it's a thrilling challenge for them to see if they can con you back into a relationship with them. And they SUCCEED at this all the time. You need to be very aware of that, because unless you truly heal (especially from trauma bonding), you will always be vulnerable to being hoovered back in again.

I recommend going No Contact on SM first. That's basically any contact you might have on your phone or any other device. Do it because if you don't, you're leaving the door wide open for the Narc to come slithering back in, and they will.

Let's have a look at some very common hoovering tactics and see how they usually show up post-discard and what you can do to protect yourself from further abuse.

Social Media Hoovering

Text messages will start showing up. The Romantic Predator will send you sweet messages, saying things like:

'I know things got rough towards the end, but I want you to know how much you really mean to me. I just felt I had to tell you that.'

This can have a huge emotional punch if you are still in love (and Trauma Bonded) with your Ex – or at least, the idea of who he/she was. You'll immediately be transported back to those golden days when everything was fabulous... the very act of remembering it brings the longing for it into powerful focus and it can be very very difficult to ignore or delete the message.

But you MUST delete the message. Block sender. Do it before you have a chance to change your mind. This is a manipulation tactic. Nothing more. They don't care about you. They didn't back then, they proved that in spades and they don't now. All they are after is narcissistic supply. Don't give it to them. If you're struggling with this, immediately switch the picture in your head from the golden days, to the reality of what went on during the devaluing stage. Recall with crystal clarity how the Narc made you feel during that time, and really feel into it. Then fast forward to the discard stage... and recall that in all its painful detail too. Remember how you really FELT.

Now ask yourself, do you want to go through that again? Because as sure as DAY IS DAY and NIGHT is NIGHT, you WILL have to go through it again and worse, if you allow the Narc back into your life. So hit the delete. Block the sender. Do this across all your SM so they can't send you any messages - at all!

Another type of tactic the Ex might use is they completely overlook the reality of what they did to you, sending you a text along the lines of 'Hey you, long time! What's going on? What are you up to these days?' You might wonder if they intended to send this to you or sent it by mistake. Surely, they can't have sent you this innocuous message after all they did to you? Then you'll think 'WTF? Is he/she kidding me?' You might be enraged and think 'I'm going to give him/her a piece of my mind...' and you start typing up your reply.

My advice here is: Don't! If you do, you're immediately giving them fuel and that's what they want and need from you. Don't give them the satisfaction. That's not all. If you do reply, you've opened up the dialogue channel and given them a golden opportunity to spout forth all kinds of new bullshit specifically designed to ensnare you. Remember they know all your weak spots and they'll aim to push all your emotional buttons to feel sorry for them, forgive them and fall for them again. This is hoovering 101.

Here are some examples of hoovering ploys:

They might take the *'Oh come on, it wasn't THAT bad! Every couple has ups and downs in their relationships. Can't we put this behind us and start again?'* angle... and you just might fall for it, because you so want that 'Golden Period' back again.

They'll take the humble road... they'll tell you they've been seeing a therapist and they understand themselves so much better now and know where they went wrong...they've changed!

They'll say they've been desolate or even suicidal since you guys broke up, they're heartbroken and would give anything – anything, to turn back the clock and have you in their arms again. All of these tactics are designed to hit your emotional buttons, and it would be very easy for you to think 'Maybe they deserve a second chance'... trust me, they do NOT.

Another common ploy:

They'll fake a life-threatening illness – they've got cancer or think they're having a heart-attack or pretend one of their family is having a medical crisis and it's all designed to make you abandon what you are doing and rush to their side.

Another one is – they'll take you on a nostalgic mental trip about how great X, Y or Z was. That fabulous day at the ocean, that amazing time at the concert or the delicious food at that special restaurant, usually accompanied by a romantic picture of the two of you or a link to 'your song'. Cue the violins.

All these tactics are designed to push your emotional buttons. They know how. Your job is to know exactly what they're up to and let it fall off you like water off a duck's back. Basically, a narcissist will tell every lie known to humankind and try every tactic in the book – just to suck you back in. Those are just a very few examples – but the crux of it is, no matter what they say, you can't believe a single word of it because they are pathological liars. They're only doing this to suck you back in and start the cycle of abuse all over again. Anything they say or do post-discard is nothing more than another of their manipulation tactics. Even if they send you a message 'by mistake'... know it was no mistake. It's just another ploy. Please don't fall for it!

In Person

That takes care of SM, but they don't stop there. They can and will arrange to 'bump' into you if you're still living in the same area, because they'll know all your favorite hangouts, your work location, schedule and pretty much everything about your usual movements. Or they'll get their flying monkeys involved, to coerce you back.

Suicide threats

They will even threaten suicide (this can be done in person or via texts/phone calls). This is more likely to come from a vulnerable narcissist given their personality profile – it's far less likely to happen with an Elite narcissist, who will have far more sophisticated ways of hoovering you back up. Suicide threats, however, are a form of emotional blackmail of the highest order and you will be so terrified of this happening, you will give in and take them back. The mainstream narrative seems to be that narcissists don't commit suicide because they are too selfish. I even believed this to be the case myself until researching more for this book. Although more often than not, suicide threats ARE just another form of deep narcissistic manipulation, narcissists DO commit suicide. The threat may not be empty.

However, what you need to understand and deeply internalize is if someone commits suicide, it is his or her choice. If they decide to take the final step to ending their lives, it is no one's fault but their own. You are not to blame. You didn't kill them. You are not responsible for anyone's life (with the exception of children under your care and protection of course). Don't let yourself be terrified by this threat, should you ever hear it. If you do and you have reason to believe they might carry it out, contact someone who knows them and tell them of your concerns. Ask that person to talk to them and help them get help. Do NOT be tempted to rush in and save them yourself.

Coming back to hoovering in person. To a degree, you're stuck because you may not want to move job, house or stop using your fave hangouts, but I know people who have done ALL of these things to cut contact with a persistent Ex and you may have to. If your Ex keeps turning up and threatens you or you fear for your safety, report it to the police and get a restraining order if that's what it takes. I know women who've had to do this too. But those are last resorts, so let's have a look at what you can do if your Ex turns up at your usual hangouts before it gets to those stages, because not ALL situations lead to your having to take such radical action.

Plan ahead and play the scene in your mind

What will help you immensely pre-planning, so sit down and think about all the possible places you might run into your Ex. When I say 'ex, that doesn't just mean ex-partner – this applies to any Narc you have gone 'No contact' with. Think about where they might turn up - even totally implausible places and imagine the scene in your head. See yourself carrying out these different scenarios I'm going to talk about in a minute.

Also, imagine the scenario where you run into your ex-partner and he's with his or her shiny new supply. Picture that too so you'll be ready for it, it won't send you into a tailspin and you can evade them as quickly as possible.

Write out a few 'Instant/Escape' Phrases

Next, write out a few 'instant' phrases that you can say in any given situation and practice them so they sound real and comfortable coming out of your mouth. Forewarned is forearmed as they say and this is one of the best mental preps you can possibly do to cover yourself in the event you do run into your nasty Ex.

Be Alert and Ready for action

When you're out and about, scan your surroundings, but always be decisive and focused on where you are going. If you have trusted friends (who are NOT friends with the narc, this is absolutely critical) get them to keep their eyes out for you too. Once inside the venue – coffee shop, restaurant or whatever, sit where you can see the door. If the Narc enters, avert your eyes. Arrange to swap seats with one of your friends so your back will now be facing the Narc's direction.

If your Ex approaches with a big smile and 'Hi, how's it going?' say politely or blandly 'Great' or 'Ok' and look back to your friend or friends. Have them well prepped about your ex, so they can be sure to pick up the conversation quickly so you are drawn straight back into their conversation and this excludes the Narc. They will generally get the message as they're unlikely to want to stand there making a fool of themselves. This is not comfortable for the Narc. Remember, they need to be the center of attention and denying them this makes them shrivel inside.

If you're dining alone, exercise the same caution by facing the door. Try to sit in a very open area surrounded by other diners. This gives the Narc less chance to start harassing you or smooth-talking you if there are a lot of ears around you. Again, keep your answers bland and divert your attention to your food. You could say 'Sorry I can't talk – I've got to be out of here soon'. Again, if you start eating and ignoring your ex, he's unlikely to stand there sticking out like a sore thumb.

If your Ex sits down – and they might, keep calm and keep eating. They'll probably talk, but if you're busy eating, YOU can't say anything and the 'chewing time' will also buy you time to think of a measured response. Responses need to be bland, bland, bland... Oscar-winningly, grey-rockingly bland! Say as little as possible. Let them talk... respond with the odd 'Hmmm'.... Or 'Yeah....' Mono syllables all the way.

RESIST the urge to engage in conversation. Don't answer any direct questions. Don't think you've got to be polite. You don't owe this person ANYTHING! Finish your meal, pay and get out. Dash off to an imaginary appointment.

Here are a few other suggestions I've found by researching on YouTube myself, and they're all sensible and workable:

Wear headphones... even if you're not listening to anything. Keep your eye out for them and pretend you haven't seen them. If they call out to you, ignore them. You wouldn't hear them if you had music playing, but they won't know that you're just pretending to listen.

Keep moving... keep going where you were going and don't get sidetracked by their attempts to stop you... don't be reactive, just be in a hurry and keep moving. If you've practiced a few phrases already as I've suggested, they should spring to mind pretty quickly and you just say them and keep going.

If they do come up in front of you... keep your body turned away from them – hips and feet away from them – this body language shuts them out without you having to say anything – and of course, as I've said, trot out your escape phrase!

If you're stopped dead in front of them and feel trapped... have your escape line or phrase at the ready – say 'Wow...' look at your watch and suddenly remember you have an appointment – say a breezy 'hey! I'm late for an appointment! Gotta go' and get out of there fast.

The key is to be as un-reactive to THEM as possible... you're the one in control and it's vital for you to remember this. Your reaction is what they are craving and you don't have to give it to them. Remember you don't owe them anything. They've taken enough already and vow that they are not going to take anything more from you.

Remember the reality

The point of doing these things is to help you to stop feeling and acting like a victim. Know that you have power and there are things you can do to help yourself feel stronger. Aside from those practical steps you can take to protect yourself from hoovering, as I've stated in this book, the most powerful form of protection you can have is to stand in your own truth and knowledge of what they did to you. **Remember the reality** of what they put you through and know without a shadow of a doubt if you go back, you are going to enter the gates of hell once more.

Then, you will suffer even more because you'll feel betrayed all over again, you'll feel so stupid you fell for their lies again. You'll be embarrassed and ashamed to admit to family and friends what you've done and they'll be furious with you if you do tell them and this will further isolate you from them. You'll begin lying and hiding the truth of what's going on. You'll dig yourself more deeply into the pit than ever and it'll become even more difficult to get out. Eventually you'll burn all your bridges and you'll be left stranded on an island of hopelessness and despair. This might sound like something out of a Dystopian Novel, but it's the reality I'm hearing about from people every day. When you're faced with a potential hoovering situation, remember, with crystal clarity, the reality.

Red Flag No 49: Love-Bombed, Devalued, Discarded… AGAIN

We've come full circle, and I wanted to remind you of all you've been through and what you'll have to go through AGAIN if you allow yourself to be Hoovered back in. You've BEEN there, done that, got the ABUSE T-Shirt, you're still suffering the trauma of the abuse and now you're about to walk straight back into the lion's den. But this time it will be so much worse.

There is a huge bouquet of red roses staring at you, the beautiful scent filling the room. Now do you go all soft, gooey and forgiving inside or do you notice the yellow Narcissus sitting snugly amidst the roses? Keep a copy of this book on your bookshelf, or as a screensaver or wallpaper on your phone, and if you are ever tempted, look at it. Open it. Read again the Red Flags which resonated most with your situation. Let it be a reminder to you you are NEVER going to let this happen to you again. Think 'Red Flag No 49: Never Again

Red Flag No 50: You've lost yourself but you can find YOU again

I hear this time and again from people who contact me. They tell me they used to be so confident, outgoing, happy, they used to be fun, kind, caring, they used to love connecting with people and were always excited about life.

Now, after being systematically and callously abused for so long, they feel lost, isolated, depressed, joyless, angry, hurt, and even suicidal. They have little interest in anything and are just getting through the day as best they can. They say they don't know who they are anymore, they feel they have lost themselves and will never find themselves again.

Here is a message that just popped into my messenger as I was writing this:

'I don't recognize myself. My depression and anxiety is the worst. I can't function at all. I've been finding myself talking to myself for hours. Or pinching or scratching myself. I am a complete mess and feel so alone.'

This woman is in so much emotional pain she is pinching and scratching herself to try and deal with the pain. This can devolve into cutting/self-harming. What happens with self-harming is that when one is experiencing overwhelming emotional pain they cannot bear, they cut or injure their body as a way of diverting their attention away *from* the emotional and *to* the physical pain. It can also be used as a form of self-punishment, that is how damaging this form of abuse can be. If you are reading this and you are self-harming, I urge you to contact a professional who can help you.

It makes me so angry what these hateful narcissists have done to them. I do believe narcissists are inherently evil and that they will eventually pay for their willful, vicious, malignant inflicting of pain onto good kind people. I'm a great believer in Karma and what goes around comes around, if not in this life, then in the next. You cannot get off scot free in the great scheme of the cosmos. You will have to pay by suffering yourself and they will eventually pay by their own suffering because that is how Karma works. It metes out total justice in its own way. You cannot willfully hurt another person and not pay the price one day yourself. Take comfort in that knowledge.

But in the meantime, I tell the people who contact me that they have NOT lost themselves. The self that they knew is still hiding inside, waiting to be found again. I advise them – and advise you now too, to tune into yourself and reconnect with who you are. Reignite the spark of joy and let it begin to burn again. Let it guide you out of the darkness, towards that light at the end of the tunnel. Healing starts with self-love.

I want to ask you a question now, and it's an important one.

Why don't you love yourself enough? Pause here and really think about this.

Did anything interesting come up for you? This may be the first time you have ever considered this question, so don't worry if it scares you, or you have no idea how to answer it, but make a note of your response. Somewhere inside you lies the answer and this question is planting a seed in you that will start to grow. It is the genesis for your healing journey to begin.

You got involved with a narcissist and it was not your fault, but there was a reason it happened to you. Something or someone made you feel the way you were treated was acceptable. Maybe it was your childhood, but you've never connected the dots. Maybe it was being bullied at school or maybe something happened to you later in life that made you vulnerable.

For whatever reason, your sense of self took the greatest battering of its life when you became entangled with a narcissist. You couldn't possibly have known what lay in store. In whatever way your self-love was damaged, it is important for you to know that you can learn to love yourself enough to never accept any kind of abuse again. If your inner child is self-conscious, hurting, sad and scared, you can start your healing journey now, with that seed. Remember that mighty oaks from little acorns grow, and I want that little acorn in you to become the mighty oak of who you are truly meant to be.

When that seed grows and flourishes, you will forever know that you are lovable and deserving of being treated with love and respect. What happened to you in the past was not your fault, but the decision to heal and re-direct your life is within your control now. It is all up to you. Any day is a good day to start taking back your power and control over your life.

Realizing this, and coming to understanding and accepting it, is a big step, but it's at the core of everything, across the board of narcissistic abuse as far as I'm concerned. If you loved yourself unconditionally and had infinite self-worth you would never, ever have become a target or a victim of a narcissist. You'd send them packing at the first sign of disrespect. If you take in as much as you can from this book, you will never become a target again.

And I reiterate, healing IS possible for YOU, and it does not have to take years. Start now, when you finish this book and try to find a way to really tune into yourself. Decide to take your life back. Decide you are done with being a victim. Decide you are going to take your power back. Your healing will begin the moment you decide you have had enough and you are going to do whatever it takes to start healing. Healing is a process, a journey, but as the saying goes, a 1000-mile journey starts with the first step and your decision that enough is enough is your first step.

The key to deep healing is, ultimately, self-love. I realize that is also a journey you have to take and you can't get there overnight. But you can start taking small steps towards that destination. Decide you are good enough. Just try saying, 'I'm good enough!' Say it several times a day. Drown out the voice saying you're not. Decide you deserve love. Just try saying it: 'I deserve love'. It might feel awkward but that's ok. The more awkward it feels, the closer you are to the truth of what is really going on inside of you.

Decide you are worth spending time with, just you, yourself and you lol! Because you ARE. If you believe in a Higher Power, try spending a few minutes every day tuning in and asking for guidance and strength to heal. And don't give up on you. EVER! Don't let the narcissist take one more moment of joy from you. The best revenge you can take on a narcissist is to be happy.

If you can learn to love and value yourself for the unique person you are, you'll never be a victim of any kind of abuse, ever again. That is what is going to protect you and make you completely bullet-proof more than anything else. It starts with loving, respecting, and valuing yourself and when you reach that stage you will never fall into a Romantic Predator's trap again.

CONCLUSION

I hope with all my empathetic heart this book has helped you to understand the danger lurking out there in the form of the Romantic Predator and their Lieutenants. I hope learning what to look for helps you spot them so fast, you can walk away from them with a smile in your heart, knowing you've honed your Narc Radar to the point that you're now a Narc Sleuth. You slay them simply by not being an available target.

But don't give up on love! Whist there are too many narcissists out there for anyone's liking, there are also millions of honest, healthy, happy people who are looking for real, loving relationships. You can have love and a fulfilling sex life with a nice man (or woman) if that's what you are looking for, no matter what your age. They are out there, and you have to start putting your focus on what that would look like for you. Believe in it and don't give up on finding Mr. or Ms. Nice who's also hot between the sheets! There seems to be a perception with many of the women I've talked to that they can't have exciting, fulfilling sex with a 'nice' guy. This is a false construct, a limiting belief they are holding in their heads and it is partly the reason why they are attracting narcissists. They have subconsciously internalized this 'bad boy' image and think they'll only get good sex with a bad boy. The sad truth is of course, when you end up with a narcissist, the sex, as I've demonstrated in Flag No 35, is absolutely abysmal.

What will also happen as you learn to love and respect yourself more is that you will start vibrating at a different level. You will be giving out a different kind of energy, one that will naturally repel potential predators and if your desire is to meet a good, decent, kind, genuine person to fall in love with, then that is what you can attract. Visualize yourself meeting someone who embodies all the genuine qualities that you are looking for in a partner and give it out to the Universe, with joy, expectation and gratitude. Let it go and allow the Universe to do the work for you. I wish you joy and love!

CONNECT WITH MARIA

Do you need more help and support to heal from narcissistic abuse?

If so then I recommend you take a look at my new book, Narcissistic Abuse Healing: The No-B.S. Guide to Healing in Weeks, Not Years. You can check it out here:

https://www.narcissist icabuse-healing.com/the-no-bs-guide-to-healing-book

Come and join my Facebook Groups

If you are looking to connect with others who have been through narcissistic abuse, I invite you to join my Facebook Support Group/s. Here's how you can do that:

Women Only
https://www.facebook.com/groups/infiniteselfworthafternarcissi st icabuse/

Men Only
https://www.facebook.com/groups/narcissist icabuserecoveryformen/

Mixed Group for Parental Alienation
https://www.facebook.com/groups/coparentingwithnarcissists

My YouTube Channel

I have over 100 Videos on my Channel, where I discuss various aspects of narcissistic abuse and Recovery

https://www.youtube.com/c/Narcissist
icAbuseHealingwithMariaMcMahon

Working with me

If you are really struggling and need a therapist who can help, I offer a free 30-minute 'Crisis to Clarity' Session to explore the possibility of working together. If you'd like to talk to me, you can book a session by clicking here:

https://book1-2-1-withmaria.as.me/

My website is www.narcissist icabuse-healing.com

For any feedback or comments, you can email me at mariamcmahoncoach@gmail.com

A Special Gift for you!

I've long been a fan of hypnosis and meditation recordings and have created some very special 'Cogni-Fusion' recordings. My Cogni-Fusion recordings have between 3 to 7 layers of different recordings. These may be combinations of music, nature, suggestions, NLP metaphors/therapy, subliminal messages and Brainwave Entrainment. For best results I recommend you listen when you will not be disturbed and can fully engage with the experience. Repeated listening is also highly recommended for faster results.

This MP3, Supreme Self-Confidence, is Ideal for:

Raising your self-esteem
Feeling much more positive
Increasing your confidence levels

Everyone deserves to have a strong sense of self-worth and value. Feeling great about yourself starts on the inside. By changing the negative internal dialogue, you can reprogram your mind to feel instantly more confident. The recording includes a powerful 'release your limiting beliefs' exercise which will help you let go of emotional issues that no longer serve you. This recording will also flood your subconscious mind with powerful subliminal affirmations that will fire up your self-esteem and have your confidence levels soaring day by day.

It's a wonderful 5-layer recording!

Layer 1: Nature Sounds
Layer 2: Ambient Music
Layer 3: Relaxation Induction, positive suggestion, ego strengthening and post hypnotic suggestion.
Layer 4: Cleaning & Releasing Technique Therapy
Layer 5: 500 repeated subliminal affirmations

Running Time: 44 Minutes

Don't listen whilst driving or operating machinery!

To get your free gift, click here: https://www.narcissisticabuse-healing.com/supreme-self-confidence-mp3-gift

Final Words and a poem especially for you

I've always said it takes a very strong person to deal with, survive and thrive after narcissistic abuse, but I am delighted to say it's happening every day. Men and women just like you are healing and taking back their power and their lives. They woke up and decided, yes **decided**, to refuse to live one more day feeling worthless and devalued. They found the courage to fight back, to find themselves and to redefine their own worth. No matter how you might be feeling right now, know that you can too.

I'd like to leave you with this... a little poem wrote for you.

Don't look back

Let your tears fall like rain
let those tears wash away your pain
Let your heart break in two
then start rebuilding a brand new you

Let your hurt be your friend
knowing that love was just pretend
Let your pain swell like the ocean
knowing the cause was a toxic love potion

You didn't deserve this brutal act
you thought you'd made a lifelong pact
You couldn't have known the depth of deceit
about to be laid down at your feet

Forgive yourself for not seeing through
just what a narcissist could do
They falsely captured your loving heart
then totally tore it wide apart

It took time and it took grief

you worked so hard to find relief
They tried so hard to tear you down
But in the end, you didn't drown

Search deep inside to find what's real
that part of you they couldn't steal
You have a strength they couldn't break
it's over now, no more heartache

Walk away with your head held high
spread your wings, now you can fly
Don't look back, don't live with regret
but remember what you must never forget
Maria McMahon

ABOUT THE AUTHOR

'Knowledge is Power!'

Maria McMahon specializes in narcissistic abuse recovery and works with people from all over the world to help them overcome the horrendous fallout from this toxic form of abuse. The Top 50 Red Flags of Romantic Predators: How to avoid the Narcissist's Trap is her first book on Narcissism. She believes 'Knowledge is Power' and the more you know about Narcissism, the better you can protect yourself from becoming a victim.

Maria also believes that you can heal from the abuse in weeks, not years, and her second book, 'Narcissistic Abuse Healing: The No-B.S. Guide to Healing in Weeks, Not Years', goes into how and why that is possible. You can check out her new book here:

https://www.narcissist icabuse-healing.com/the-no-bs-guide-to-healing-book

You can find out more at www.infiniteselfworth.com

She also runs two narcissistic abuse support groups, one for men and one for women, on Facebook and you are welcome to join, but please answer the questions or you will not be approved. This is done to protect the groups from trolls / narcs. Yes, they do try to infiltrate groups.

Women Only
https://www.facebook.com/groups/infiniteselfworthafternarcissi st icabuse/

Men Only
https://www.facebook.com/groups/narcissist icabuserecoveryformen/

Her interests include psychology, neuroscience, brainwave entrainment, self-help, spirituality, cosmology and life in general. Maria was certified in Clinical NLP/Hypnotherapy in London in 1993, and obtained her BSc in Psychology in 1996. In 2014 she also qualified in Life Coaching.

Maria also runs a Facebook Books Group: Self-Help, Spirituality and Wellness Books, which currently has over 5,500 members. Authors and readers are all welcome.

You can join here:
https://www.facebook.com/groups/selfhelpspiritualbooks

Maria is also author of 'Law of Attraction Shortcut Secrets', 'A Pocketful of Thank You', and co-author with Else Byskov of 3 Books in the spiritual 'Nutshell Series':

'Reincarnation in a Nutshell'.
'Fate and Karma in a Nutshell'
'Life after Death in a Nutshell'
All are available on Amazon.

Apart from her love of spirituality and personal development, she's always loved travel and international culture. Over the last 30 years she's lived in Germany, London, Hong Kong, Dubai, Abu Dhabi and Azerbaijan and now lives in Southern Spain. She's an ex-Catholic, animal lover, vegetarian and shares her views of the Mediterranean from her apartment with three rescue dogs, Levi, Skye and Reuben.

And finally, a BIG favor…

Thank you for reading this book. If you have enjoyed it and more importantly, found it helpful, please take a few minutes to leave a short review on your favourite book platform. Your review can help someone who is really suffering with narcissistic abuse to know whether this book will help him or her too.

And please share the link to this book on your social media, narcissistic abuse recovery groups and with anyone who you think will benefit from reading this book. The author will be very grateful to you.

Links to share the books:

Red Flags Book:
https://www.narcissist icabuse-healing.com/the-top-50-red-flags-of-romantic-predators-book

No-B.S. Guide to Healing:
https://www.narcissist icabuse-healing.com/the-no-bs-guide-to-healing-book

READING AND RESOURCES LIST

I've broken this down into an 'easy find' format, in case you want to do further research for yourself.

Experts on Narcissistic abuse

These authors are all extremely good and provide a lot of valuable information on NPD, abuse and recovery, via their books, blogs and YouTube Channels. I've listed some of the books of theirs I've read and they are all excellent, and available on the major book platforms.

Arabi, Shahida
Becoming the Narcissist's Nightmare: How to Devalue the Narcissist While Supplying Yourself.

Durvasula, Ramani, PhD
Should I stay or Should I Go? Surviving a Relationship with a Narcissist

Evans, Melanie Tonia
You Can Thrive After Narcissistic Abuse: The #No 1 System for Recovering from Toxic Relationships

Saeed, Kim
How To Do No Contact Like A Boss!: The Woman's Guide To Implementing No Contact and Detaching from Toxic Relationships

Ryan, Evelyn M.
Take Your Power Back: Healing Lessons, Tips, and Tools for Abuse Survivors

Tudor, HG
Red Flag: 50 Warning Signs of Narcissistic Seduction

Tudor, HG
Sitting Target: How and Why the Narcissist Chooses You

Vaknin, Sam
Malignant Self-Love: Narcissism Revisited (FULL TEXT, 10th Edition, 2015)

Survivors of Narcissistic abuse Authors

These are some of the authors who have survived narcissistic abuse and gone on to write their own books about the experience.

Hurts, T Ruth
My Narcissistic ex-boyfriend: How I recovered from Mental abuse (The book gives a very good window into how narcissists operate long-term to ensnare you. You'll have to forgive the grammar in places.)

Lethbridge, C
UNMASKED: Surviving Narcissistic Abuse

Miller, Lee and Lee, Michelle (Editor)
Dating Harley Quinn: My 3 Years with A Female Narcissist

Williams, Susan
1) Planet Ben: Inside the World of a Narcissist (The Love Games Book 1)
2) End of the Fairytale: Letting go of the Narcissist (The Love Games Book 2)
3) Titanium: Strength After A Narcissist (The Love Games Book 3)

Neuroscience and Brain Chemicals

Bathla, Som
Build A Happier Brain: The Neuroscience and Psychology of Happiness. Learn Simple yet Effective Habits for Happiness in

Personal, Professional Life and Relationships (Power-Up Your Brain Book 5)

Graziano Breuning, Loretta
Meet Your Happy Chemicals: Dopamine, Endorphin, Oxytocin, Serotonin

Other Resources (Web Links)

The Dopamine Diaries – From Abuse to Recovery Facebook Group
https://www.facebook.com/groups/2114655428767890/

HG Tudor
'The Greater Narcissist – Five Facts'
https://narcsite.com/2017/01/13/the-greater-narcissist -five-facts/

Bree Bonchay, LCSW
Narcissistic Abuse Affects Over 158 Million People in the U.S.
https://psychcentral.com/lib/narcissist ic-abuse-affects-over-158-million-people-in-the-u-s/

Sandra L. Brown, M.A.
60 Million People in the U.S. Negatively Affected by Someone Else's Pathology
https://www.psychologytoday.com/us/blog/pathological-relationships/201008/60-million-people-in-the-us-negatively-affected-someone-elses

Foods that Release Dopamine

Sara Lienard, Health Editor, BBC – Good Food
What is the dopamine diet?
https://www.bbcgoodfood.com/howto/guide/what-dopamine-diet

Light Therapy Boxes

Mayo Clinic
https://www.mayoclinic.org/diseases-conditions/seasonal-affective-disorder/in-depth/seasonal-affective-disorder-treatment/art-20048298

National Health Service (NHS) UK
https://www.nhs.uk/conditions/seasonal-affective-disorder-sad/
https://www.nhs.uk/conditions/seasonal-affective-disorder-sad/treatment/

DSM-5 Personality Disorders
https://www.psychiatry.org/patients-families/personality-disorders/what-are-personality-disorders

Laughter

Bourg Carter, Sherrie, Psy.D.
The Natural High of Laughter, Psychology Today
https://www.psychologytoday.com/us/blog/high-octane-women/201111/the-natural-high-laughter

Narcissistic Parents/Parenting

Karyl McBride Ph.D,: Psychology Today
The Real Effect of Narcissistic parenting on Children
https://www.psychologytoday.com/us/blog/the-legacy-distorted-love/201802/the-real-effect-narcissist ic-parenting-children

PsychAlive: The Problem with Narcissistic Parents
https://www.psychalive.org/the-problem-with-narcissist ic-parents/

Goop: The Legacy of a Narcissistic Parent
https://goop.com/work/relationships/the-legacy-of-a-narcissist ic-parent/

ScaryMommy: Narcissistic Parents Are Literally Incapable Of Loving Their Children
https://www.scarymommy.com/narcissist ic-parents-incapable-loving-children/

Self Care Haven (Shahida Arabi's Website - various articles)
https://selfcarehaven.wordpress.com/category/children-of-narcissist ic-parents/

Centers for Disease Control and Prevention
Adverse Childhood Experiences (ACEs)
https://www.cdc.gov/violenceprevention/childabuseandneglect/acestudy/index.html

Domestic Abuse / Violence Helplines

These are just some of the available helplines. If you need help, and your country is not listed, Google Domestic Abuse or Violence Helpline or Support, in your country. If you are in danger, please reach out to someone who can help you.

https://www.thehotline.org/ (United States)

https://www.womensaid.org.uk/information-support/helpline/ (United Kingdom)

https://www.lifeline.org.au/ (Australia)

http://www.awhl.org/our-mission (Canada)

https://ec.europa.eu/justice/saynostopvaw/helpline.html (Europe) - some data may be out of date and further research might be necessary to find the correct information for relevant countries.

Asia / Middle East

https://ec.europa.eu/justice/saynostopvaw/helpline.html (Pakistan)

https://www.pcw.gov.ph/directory/vaw-hotlines (Philippines)

Middle Eastern and Afghan Women (UK based)

http://ikwro.org.uk/about-us/ourservices/advice-for-women-and-girls

Printed in Great Britain
by Amazon

27754941R00155